A REALLY
SHORT
HISTORY
OF NEARLY
EVERYTHING

Originally published in Great Britain as *A Short History of Nearly Everything* by Doubleday, an imprint of Transworld Publishers,
a division of the Random House Group Limited, London, and subsequently published in the United States by
Broadway Books, an imprint of Random House, Inc., New York, in 2003. This newly illustrated, abridged, and adapted
edition was originally published in Great Britain by Doubleday, an imprint of Random House Children's Books,
a division of the Random House Group Limited, London, in 2008.

Visit us on the Web! www.randomhouse.com/kids

Educators and librarians, for a variety of teaching tools, visit us at www.randomhouse.com/teachers

Library of Congress Cataloging-in-Publication Data is available upon request.
ISBN: 978-0-385-73810-1
Abridged and edited by Felicia Law (Diverta Ltd)
Illustrations by Yuliya Somina
Additional illustrations by Martin Sanders
Initial design by Simon Webb; additional design by Margaret Hope
Subject consultants: Sarah Chant; Martin Weaver
Illustration credits can be found on page 169.

MANUFACTURED IN CHINA

10 9 8

First U.S. Edition

Bill Bryson
A REALLY SHORT HISTORY OF NEARLY EVERYTHING

DELACORTE PRESS

CONTENTS

Foreword   1

LOST IN THE COSMOS

How do they know that? – finding out about our planet   2

Cooking up a universe – recipe for an explosion   4

The Big Bang – what came next   6

Hi! Glad you could make it! – how *did* you get here?   8

Listening to the Big Bang – cosmic radiation and you   10

To the edge of the universe – how far is it?   12

Journey into space – our vast solar system   14

Looking for Pluto – the new dwarf planet   16

Journey's end – the *Voyager* expeditions   18

Who's out there? – advanced life elsewhere in the cosmos?   20

The supernova searcher – the amazing Reverend Bob Evans   22

THE SIZE OF THE EARTH

Back on Earth – Newton and gravity   24

Measuring the Earth – finding the circumference   26

Earth's bulge – our planet is not a sphere   28

How far round? – two ill-fated measuring expeditions   30

Tracking Venus – following the Venus transit   32

Weighing the Earth – gravity and Shiehallion   34

Featherweight measures – Cavendish's calculations   36

Finding Earth's age – the new science of geology   40

The stone-breakers – the Geological Society   42

Slow and steady does it – Lyell and tectonic plates   44

Finding fossils – mapping Britain's rock layers   46

Dating the rocks – the great eras of geological time   48

Tooth and claw – digging up strange bones   50

Dinosaur hunters – 'terrible lizards'   52

It's bone time – bones and Earth's age   54

The mighty atom – Dalton weighs atoms   56

A matter of chemistry – adding to the elements   58

The Periodic Table – Mendeleyev instils some order   60

Glowing elements – Marie Curie and deadly radiation   62

A NEW AGE DAWNS

Einstein – the genius – the Special Theory of Relativity   64

Spacetime – time has a shape   66

The big picture – the Hubble Space Telescope   68

'Bad' science – lead and CFCs   70

A meteoric age – measuring meteorites   72

DANGEROUS PLANET

Travelling trilobites – Pangaea and the fossil record   76

Crust crunching – the discovery of tectonic plates   78

All adrift – where does all the sediment go?   80

The fire below – the Earth beneath our feet   82

Boom! – the eruption of Mount St Helens   84

Yellowstone Park – a volcano in waiting   86

Big quakes – measuring earthquakes   88

Impact from space – meteors and the KT extinction   90

Asteroid hit – rocky objects heading for us?   92

LIFE ITSELF

Our tiny patch – a comfortable place to be   94

Earth's blanket – the atmosphere that protects us   96

Wild and windy – Earth's weather   98

Hot-water bottle – the effect of the oceans   100

Awash with water – a watery planet   102

Down in the deep – living on the ocean floor   104

Protein soup – oceans – where life started   106

Battling bacteria – the coming of microbes   108

Your mini world – the bacteria that feed on us   110

Making you ill – infectious organisms   112

Citizen cells – you and your cells   116

How long can you stay? – adapt or die   118

A runaway success – trilobites and other fossils   120

Time to get started – Earth's long pre-human history   122

Out of the sea – when creatures took to the land 124

Where did we come from? – from reptiles to mammals 126

Comings and goings – the great extinctions 128

Labelling life – the classification of plants and animals 130

Can't count? – Earth's unknown creatures 132

Journey to the future – Darwin and *On the Origin of Species* 134

The quiet monk – Mendel and the study of genes 136

One big happy family – inheritance and chromosomes 138

Chain of life – Crick and Watson and DNA 140

THE ROAD TO US

Hot and cold – ice sheets and climate 142

Chilly times – living in an ice age 144

Skull and bones – discovering early human remains 146

Lucy – the most famous australopithecine 148

From there to here – the rise of *Homo sapiens* 150

Tool-makers – inventors of the first technology 152

Humans take over – extermination and extinction 156

What now? – a polluted planet 158

Goodbye – our planet and us 160

Index 162

Picture credits 169

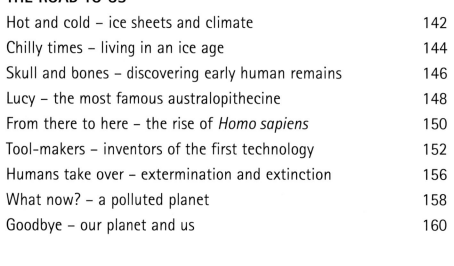

Foreword

Have you ever closed your eyes and tried to imagine just how big infinity is? Or wondered what there used to be before there was a universe? Or tried to envision what it would be like to travel at the speed of light or peer into a black hole?

And did all this make your brain hurt a little? Well, don't worry, I am here to help you. I spent about fifty years asking myself brain-straining questions and finally decided (because I don't move very fast) to see if I couldn't find some answers. You are holding the result.

All that has changed with this special new edition is that it is much shorter – though the best bits are all still in – and cunningly illustrated to make it easy to see exactly how this universe of ours is put together.

I learned two particular things from doing this book. The first is that there isn't anything in existence – not a thing – that isn't amazing and interesting when you look into it. Whether you are talking about how the universe began from nothing, or how each one of us is made up of trillions of mindless atoms that somehow work together in an agreeably coordinated fashion, or why the oceans are salty, or what happens when stars explode, or anything at all – it is all amazingly interesting. It really is.

The other thing I learned is that we are just awfully lucky to be here. In the entire unimaginable sprawl of the universe, just one small speck of a planet has life on it, as far as we know – and we get to come from that planet. You and I and a few billion other lucky organisms may be the only things anywhere that can get up and move around and talk and think and see and do. When you have had that kind of good fortune, it's only natural to say to yourself: 'How did that happen?'

Well, turn the page and come with me now, and we'll see if we can't find out.

Bill Bryson

How do they know that?

Me at elementary school, USA.

This is a book about how IT happened – in particular, how we went from there being nothing at all to there being something. And then, how a little of that something turned into us, and also some of what happened in between – and since.

My own starting point, for what it's worth, was a science book that I had when I was in fourth or fifth grade at American elementary school. It was a standard issue 1950s schoolbook – battered, unloved, heavy – but near the front it had an illustration that just captivated me: a cutaway diagram showing the Earth's interior as it would look if you cut into the planet with a large knife and carefully withdrew a wedge representing about a quarter of its bulk.

I clearly remember being transfixed. I suspect my interest was based on the horrifying image in my mind of streams of unsuspecting motorists plunging over the edge of a sudden 4,000-mile-high cliff into the centre of the planet. But gradually, I did turn in a more student-like manner to the scientific meaning behind the drawing and the realization that the Earth consisted of separate layers, ending in the centre with a glowing sphere of iron and nickel, which was as hot as the surface of the Sun, according to the caption. And I remember thinking with real wonder: **How do they know that?**

It's a miracle!

I didn't doubt the correctness of the information for an instant – I still tend to trust what scientists say in the same way I trust surgeons and plumbers. But I couldn't for the life of me conceive how any human mind could work out what spaces thousands of miles below us, which no eye had ever seen and no X-ray could penetrate, could look like and be made of. **To me that was just a miracle.**

I grew up convinced that science was extremely dull – but suspecting that it needn't be.

How and why?

Excited, I took the book home that night and opened it before dinner – an action that I expect prompted my mother to feel my forehead and ask if I was all right – and, starting with the first page, I began to read. **And here's the thing. It wasn't exciting at all.**

Above all, it didn't answer any of the questions that the illustrations stirred up, such as:

- How did we end up with a sun in the middle of our planet and how do they know how hot it is?
- And if it is burning away down there, why isn't the ground under our feet hot to touch?
- And why isn't the rest of the interior melting – or is it?
- And when the core at last burns itself out, will some of the Earth slump into the void, leaving a giant sinkhole on the surface?

Who's got the answers?

The author was strangely silent on such details. It was as if he wanted to keep the good stuff secret by making all of it totally unfathomable. Then, much later – about ten years ago – I was on a long flight across the Pacific, staring idly out of the window, when it occurred to me that I didn't know the first thing about the only planet I was ever going to live on.

I also didn't know...

- what a proton was, or a protein;
- how to tell a quark from a quasar;
- how geologists could look at a layer of rock in a canyon and tell you how old it was;
- how much the Earth weighs or how old its rocks are, or what really exists in the centre;
- how and when the universe started and what it was like when it did;
- what goes on inside an atom;
- why scientists still can't predict an earthquake or even the weather.

I am very pleased to tell you that until the late 1970s, scientists didn't know the answers to these questions either. They just didn't let on that they didn't.

Cooking up a universe

So where did we come from and how did we get started? Well, when things really got going, it was all down to atoms – those minuscule particles of matter that make up everything there is. But for a very long time, there were no atoms and no universe for them to float about in. There was nothing – nothing at all anywhere – except for something unimaginably small, which scientists call a singularity. **As it happened, this was enough!**

Protons form a tiny part of the centre of an atom. They are so small that a little dib of ink like the dot on this 'i' can hold about 2,000,000,000,000, 000,000,000,000, 000,000,000,000 of them.

Recipe for cooking up a universe:

You will need:

- one proton – shrunk down to a billionth of its size;
- every last particle of matter (that's dust, gas and any other particles of material you can find) between here and the edge of creation;
- a space – much, much smaller than the extremely small proton!

Take one proton . . .

No matter how hard you try you will never be able to grasp just how tiny a proton is. It's just way too small. A proton is an infinitesimal part of an atom, which is itself, of course, an unimaginably tiny thing. Now imagine, if you can (and of course you can't), shrinking one of those protons down to a billionth of its normal size.

Add . . .

- all the particles of matter you found;
- and squeeze them into a space so infinitesimally tight that it has no dimensions at all.

Excellent! You are ready to start a universe.

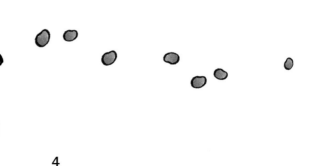

Get ready for a really BIG BANG

Naturally, you'll wish to retire to a safe place to observe the spectacle. Unfortunately, there's nowhere to retire to because surrounding your tiny, tiny mixture of ingredients, there's no 'where'. It's natural to want to think of whatever started us as a kind of dot hanging in the dark, limitless space that surrounds it. But right now there is no space and there is no darkness. Our universe will begin from nothing.

We're on our way

In a single blinding pulse, a moment of glory much too swift and dramatic to put in words, your ingredients suddenly take shape.

- The first lively second produces gravity and the other forces that govern physics.
- In less than a minute, the universe is a million billion miles across and growing fast.
- There's a lot of heat, 10 billion degrees of it, enough to begin the nuclear reactions that will eventually create the lighter elements – mainly hydrogen and helium.
- And in three minutes, 98 per cent of everything there is, or will ever be in the universe, has been produced.

We have a universe. It is a wondrous place and beautiful too. And it was all done in about the time it takes to make a sandwich.

And so, from nothing, our universe begins

Quite when this moment happened is a matter of some debate. Cosmologists have argued for a long time over whether the moment of creation was ten billion years ago or twice that, or something in between. The consensus seems to be heading for a figure of about 13.7 billion years, but these things are impossibly difficult to measure, as we shall see further on. All that can really be said is that at some unknown point in the very distant past, for reasons equally unknown, there came the moment known to science as 'time equals zero', or **t = 0**.

Before the Big Bang, time didn't exist. However, in a fraction of a split second, t would be something. Let's find out what.

The Big Bang

The Big Bang theory isn't about the bang itself but about what happened after the bang. Not long after, mind you. By doing a lot of maths, scientists believe they can look back to one ten million trillion trillion trillionths of a second after its birth when the universe was still so small that you would have needed a microscope to find it.

Here comes gravity...
At one ten-millionth of a trillionth of a trillionth of a trillionth of a second after the Big Bang, gravity emerges.

Electro-magnetism,
nuclear forces – the stuff of physics – are present in an instant.

Particles of 'stuff'
arrive from nothing at all. Suddenly there are swarms of protons, electrons, neutrons and more.

Here's our Sun
A great swirl of gas and dust some 25 billion kilometres across begins to assemble in space. Virtually all of it, 99.9 per cent in fact, goes to make up the Sun.

Here's Earth
Out of the floating material that's left over, two microscopic grains float close enough together to be joined by electrostatic forces. This is the moment our planet is born.

Although everyone calls it the Big Bang, many books tell us not to think of it as a normal kind of explosion. It was, rather, a vast, sudden expansion on a whopping scale.

'Baby' planets
All over the solar system, the same was happening. Colliding dust grains formed larger and larger clumps. Eventually, the clumps grew large enough to be called planetesimals. As these endlessly bumped and collided, they broke or split or joined up again in endless ways. But in every encounter there was a winner, and some of the winners grew big enough to dominate the orbit around which they travelled. It all happened remarkably quickly. To grow from a tiny cluster of grains to a baby planet probably took just a few tens of thousands of years.

Some big numbers!

Most of what we think we know about the early moments of the universe is thanks to an idea called 'inflation theory'. Imagine that a fraction of a moment after the dawn of creation, the universe underwent a sudden dramatic expansion, that it inflated at a huge speed. In just one million million million million millionths of a second – the universe changed from something you could hold in your hand to something at least 10,000,000,000,000,000,000,000,000 times bigger.

Here comes our Moon!

At some point, about 4.4 billion years ago, an object the size of Mars crashed into the Earth. It blew out enough material to form a second, smaller clump. Within a hundred years this had formed into the spherical rock we call our Moon. (Most of the lunar material is thought to have come from the Earth's mantle, not its core, which is why the Moon has so little iron, while Earth has lots.)

So, in a single instant . . .

we had a universe that was vast – at least a hundred billion light years across, but possibly any size up to infinite. It was perfectly laid out, ready for the creation of galaxies, those massive collections of stars, gas, dust and other matter orbiting around a single centre.

Now our atmosphere forms

When the Earth was only about a third of its present size, it was probably already beginning to create an atmosphere, mostly made up of carbon dioxide, nitrogen, methane and sulphur. Amazingly, from this poisonous stew of gases, life was able to form. Carbon dioxide is a powerful greenhouse gas and helped to hold in Earth's warmth. This was a good thing, because the Sun was a lot dimmer and cooler back then. Had we not had the benefit of carbon dioxide, the Earth might well have frozen over permanently and life might never have got started. But somehow it did.

Last, but not least, here comes us!

For the next 500 million years, the young Earth would continue to be pelted relentlessly by comets, meteors and other galactic debris. These brought water to fill the oceans and the components necessary for the formation of life. It was a truly hostile environment and yet somehow, tiny bags of chemicals twitched into life and WE WERE ON OUR WAY.

Hi! Glad you could make it!

From the moment you are born, you are nothing less than an atomic miracle. A baby weighing four kilograms will have about 400,000,000,000,000,000, 000,000,000 atoms in its body.

It's a slightly troubling fact that if you were to pick yourself apart with tweezers, one atom at a time, you would produce a mound of fine atomic dust, none of which had ever been alive but all of which had once been you.

Welcome. And congratulations. I am delighted that you could make it. Getting here wasn't easy, I know. In fact, I suspect it was a little tougher than you realize.

To begin with, for you to be here now, trillions of drifting atoms had somehow to come together in a complicated and obliging manner to create you. It's an arrangement so specialized and so particular that it has never been tried before and will only happen this once. For the next many years (we hope) these tiny particles will uncomplainingly go about the business of keeping you intact and will allow you to experience the agreeable state of actually existing.

What makes you you

Why atoms take this trouble is a bit of a puzzle. For all their devoted attention, your atoms don't actually care about you – indeed, they don't even know that you're there. For that matter, they don't even know that **they** are there. They are mindless particles, after all, and not even alive themselves. Yet somehow for as long as you exist, your atoms will have just one task in mind: to keep you you.

And now for the bad news...

The bad news is that atoms are fickle. You can't rely on them to stick around longer than they have to. Even a long human life only adds up to about 650,000 hours. And when that modest milestone flashes into view, for reasons unknown, your atoms will close you down, then silently disassemble and go off to be other things.

And that's it for you.

The miracle of life

Still, you can be grateful that it happens at all. It doesn't happen anywhere else in the universe so far as we can tell. This is decidedly odd because the atoms that so happily flock together to form living things on Earth are exactly the same atoms that just won't do it elsewhere.

However miraculous in some respects, at the level of chemistry, life is fantastically ordinary: carbon, hydrogen, oxygen and nitrogen, a little calcium, a dash of sulphur, a light dusting of other very ordinary elements – nothing you wouldn't find in any ordinary pharmacy – and that's all you need. The only thing special about the atoms that make you is that they make you. And that, of course, is **the true miracle of life**.

Without atoms there would be no water or air or rocks, no stars and planets, no distant gassy clouds or swirling nebulae. So, thank goodness for atoms.

Listening to the Big Bang

It was 1964 and two American scientists, Arno Penzias and Robert Wilson, were trying to make use of a large communications antenna owned by Bell Laboratories in New Jersey, USA. But they were troubled by a persistent background noise – a steady, steamy hiss that made any experimental work impossible. The noise came from every point in the sky, day and night, through every season.

A sound spring-clean!

For a year the young astronomers did everything they could to track down and eliminate the noise. They tested every electrical system. They rebuilt instruments, checked circuits, wiggled wires, dusted plugs. They climbed into the dish and placed duct tape over every seam and rivet. They climbed back into the dish with brooms and scrubbing brushes and carefully swept it clean of what they referred to in a later paper as 'white dielectric material', or what is known more commonly as bird droppings. Nothing they tried worked.

Meanwhile – just up the road . . .

Unknown to them, some 50 kilometres away, researchers at Princeton University were working on an idea suggested years before by the astrophysicist George Gamow: that if you looked deep enough into space, you should find some cosmic background radiation left over from the Big Bang. Gamow believed that by the time it had crossed the vastness of the cosmos the radiation would reach Earth in the form of microwaves. He had even suggested that the Bell antenna might do the job of picking this up.

An ancient light

The noise that Penzias and Wilson were hearing was, of course, the noise that Gamow had anticipated. They had found the edge of the universe, or at least the visible part of it, 150 billion trillion kilometres away. They were 'seeing' the first photons – the most ancient light in the universe – as microwaves, just as Gamow had predicted.

Tune in to the Big Bang

Incidentally, disturbance from cosmic background radiation is something we have all experienced. Tune your television to any channel it doesn't receive and about 1 per cent of the dancing static you see is accounted for by the ancient remains of the Big Bang. In fact, the next time you complain that there's nothing on TV, remember that you can always watch the birth of the universe!

Peering into the universe

Think of peering up into the depths of the universe as like looking upwards from the lobby of the Empire State Building in New York.

At the time of Wilson and Penzias's discovery, the most distant galaxies anyone had detected were on about the 40th floor. The most distant things – quasars – could be seen on about the 80th floor.

Now, the visible universe came to within a centimetre or so of the ceiling of the top floor. Suddenly scientists could see and understand a great deal more.

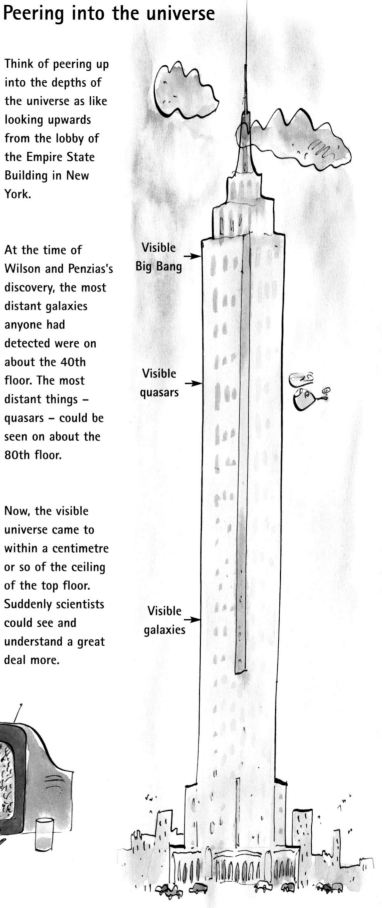

Visible Big Bang

Visible quasars

Visible galaxies

11

To the edge of the universe

Now, the question that has occurred to all of us at some point is: what would happen if you travelled right to the edge of the universe and popped your head outside? Where would your head be if it were no longer in the universe?

What edge?

The answer is disappointing – you can never get to the edge of the universe. That's because it would not only take too long to get there but, even if you travelled on and on in a straight line for ever, you would never arrive at an outer boundary. Instead, your travels would bring you right back to where you began. This is because the universe bends in a way that we can't really imagine. We are not adrift in some large, ever-expanding bubble. Rather, space curves in a way which allows it to have no actual edge or boundary, but at the same time allows it to be finite.

The visible universe is a million million million million (that's 1,000,000,000,000,000, 000,000,000) miles across.

Flat-earth man

The example that is often used to explain the way space curves is to try to imagine someone from a universe of flat surfaces, who had never seen a sphere, arriving on Earth. No matter how far they roamed across the planet's surface, they would never find an edge. They might eventually return to the spot where they'd started, and be utterly confounded to explain how that had happened.

So where are WE?

Well, we are in the same position in space as our puzzled flat-earth man, only we're flummoxed by a further question – where are **WE** in all this? Just as there's no place where you can find the edge of the universe, so there's no place where you can stand and say:
'This is where it all began. This is the centre-most point of it all.'
It would be nice to think we were at the centre of it all, and maybe we are. Scientists just can't prove it mathematically.

This isn't really surprising. After all, the universe is a huge place. For us, it reaches only as far as light has travelled in the billions of years since the universe was formed. But according to most theories, the universe is a whole lot bigger still. It's possible that the number of light years to the edge of this larger, unseen universe would be written not with ten or a hundred zeros, but with millions.

If you walked non-stop for a year, striding out at a speed of three miles an hour, you would cover a distance of 26,280 miles – or approximately once round the world. Light moves at about 670,616,629.2 miles per hour, so in the same time it will travel over six trillion miles, or 220 million times round the world.

Now let's get on board a spaceship and investigate the size of this great universe for ourselves.

KEEP GOING

FURTHER

AND FURTHER

AND FURTHER

Journey into space

Let's imagine, for purposes of entertainment, that we're about to go on a journey by rocketship. We won't go terribly far – just to the edge of our own solar system – but we need to get a fix on how big a place space is and what a small part of it we occupy.

Most schoolroom charts show the planets coming one after the other at neighbourly intervals, but this is a trick to get them all on the same piece of paper.

The solar system consists of the Sun, the eight planets, their moons, three dwarf planets, including Pluto, and their four moons, and billions of asteroids, comets, meteoroids and bits of interplanetary dust.

We'll need to get up some speed

Even at the speed of light, it would take seven hours to get to the dwarf planet of Pluto. But of course we can't travel at anything like that speed. We'll have to go at the speed of a spaceship, and these are rather more lumbering. The best speeds yet achieved by any human object are those of the *Voyager* 1 and 2 spacecrafts, which are now flying away from us at about 56,000 kilometres an hour.

Space is – well – space!

Now, the first thing you are likely to realize is that space is extremely well named and that there's not a lot going on out of the window.

Lots of empty boring space . . .

You will quickly realize that none of the maps you've ever seen of the solar system were drawn remotely to scale.

Such are the distances between the planets, in fact, that it isn't possible to do so.

Lost in space

Our solar system may be the liveliest thing for trillions of miles, but all the visible stuff in it – the Sun, the planets and their moons, the billion or so tumbling rocks of the asteroid belt, comets and other bits and pieces of drifting dust – fills less than a trillionth of the available space.

And on and on . . .

By the time we reach Pluto, we have come so far that the Sun has shrunk to the size of a pinhead. It's little more than a bright star. And you will notice as we speed past Pluto that we're not stopping. Check your itinerary and you'll see that this is a trip to the edge of our solar system and we're not nearly there yet. Pluto may be the last object marked on schoolroom charts, but the system doesn't end there. In fact, it isn't even close.

We won't get to the solar system's edge until we've passed through the Oort cloud, a vast celestial realm of drifting comets, and we won't reach the Oort cloud for another – I'm sorry to say – ten thousand years. So, the bad news, I'm afraid, is that we won't be home for supper.

Now, this may look the most boring picture ever, but it's a real photo of Earth taken by *Voyager* 1 from more than one billion miles away.

Far from marking the outer edge of the solar system, as those schoolroom maps imply, Pluto is barely one five-thousandth of the way.

and yet more boring space . . .

Even if you added lots of fold-out pages to your textbooks or used a really long sheet of poster paper, you wouldn't come close.

Next stop – Jupiter – coming up in just 300 metres (less the size of this page).

Looking for Pluto

Astronomers these days can do the most amazing things. If someone struck a match on the Moon, they could spot the flare. From the tiniest throbs and wobbles of distant stars, they can tell the size and character of planets much too remote to be seen – so distant, in fact, that it would take us half a million years in a spaceship to get there.

In short, there isn't a great deal that goes on in the universe that astronomers can't find when they have a mind to. Which is why it's all the more remarkable that until 1978, no one had noticed that Pluto had a moon.

In the summer of that year, a young astronomer named James Christy, working at the Lowell Observatory in Arizona, USA, was making a routine examination of photographic images of Pluto, when he saw that there was something blurry there, probably a moon. And it wasn't just any moon. Relative to the planet, it was the biggest moon in the solar system. Since the space occupied by the moon and the space occupied by Pluto had previously been thought to be one and the same, it meant that Pluto had to be much smaller than supposed – smaller even than Mercury. Indeed, seven other moons in our solar system, including our own, are larger than Pluto.

So why did it take so long to find a moon in our own solar system? The answer is that astronomers tend to point their instruments at very tiny little pieces of the sky, mostly looking for quasars and black holes and faraway galaxies.

With their radio telescopes astronomers can capture wisps of radiation so faint that the total amount of energy collected from outside the solar system by them all is 'less than the energy of a single snowflake striking the ground'.

We have been spoiled by artists' renderings like this one, and imagine Pluto as a clear round image. In fact, it is faint and fuzzy, and its moon is just a tiny piece of additional fuzziness.

Is it a planet?

It was the American astronomer Clyde Tombaugh who first spotted Pluto back in 1930. It was a miraculous find as Tombaugh could see at once that the new planet was very small. Even today, nobody is quite sure how big it is, what it's made of, what kind of atmosphere it has, or even what it really is.

Many astronomers questioned whether Pluto was actually a planet or merely the largest object that existed in the zone of galactic debris known as the Kuiper belt. (The Kuiper belt is the part of our solar system where short-period comets come from – those that come past pretty regularly – of which the most famous is Halley's comet.)

Expelled from the club

Finally, in 2006, Pluto was voted out of the planet league. It failed to earn the label 'planet' on several counts. Under the new rules, Pluto is classified as a 'dwarf planet'. However, having been considered a planet for over three quarters of a century, and with a NASA mission on its way and planning to arrive nearby in July 2015, Pluto won't be forgotten. So this leaves our solar system with just eight planets, four rocky inner planets and four gassy outer giants.

Tilted orbit

It's certainly true that Pluto doesn't act much like the other planets. Not only is it small and obscure, it's so changeable in its motions that no one can tell you exactly where it will be in a century. Whereas the other planets orbit on more or less the same plane, Pluto's orbit shifts out of alignment at an angle of 17 degrees, like the brim of a hat tilted on someone's head.

New rules for planets

- A planet must independently orbit the Sun;
- it must have enough mass so that gravity pulls it into a rough sphere shape;
- it must dominate its orbit; in other words, its mass must be much larger than anything else which crosses its orbit.

However, things may change again. Astronomers have now found over 600 additional Plutinos as they are called. One, Varuna, is nearly as big as Pluto's moon. They now think there may be billions of these objects. The difficulty is that many of them are awfully dark and over six billion kilometres away.

Pluto is very tiny: just one quarter of 1 per cent as massive as Earth.

Journey's end

Unfortunately, there's no chance we could ever make a journey through the solar system. A trip of 386,000 kilometres to the Moon still represents a huge undertaking. Even with the Hubble telescope, we can't see into the Oort cloud that lies out there somewhere beyond Pluto and stretches away into the cosmos.

Based on what we know now, there's absolutely no prospect that any human being will ever visit the edge of our own solar system. But if we did, our own Sun would be a distant tiny twinkle, not even the brightest star in the sky.

So now you can start to understand how even significant objects in our solar sytem – Pluto's moon, for example – have escaped attention. Until the *Voyager* expeditions, Neptune was thought to have two moons; *Voyager* found six more! Some 30 years ago, the solar system was thought to hold 30 moons. The total now is at least 90, about a third of which have been found in the last ten years.

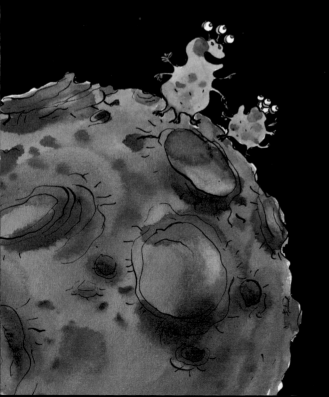

Space travel remains dangerous and costly. A manned mission to Mars was quietly dropped when someone worked out that it would cost $450 billion and probably result in the deaths of all the crew (their bodies torn to tatters by high-energy solar particles).

18

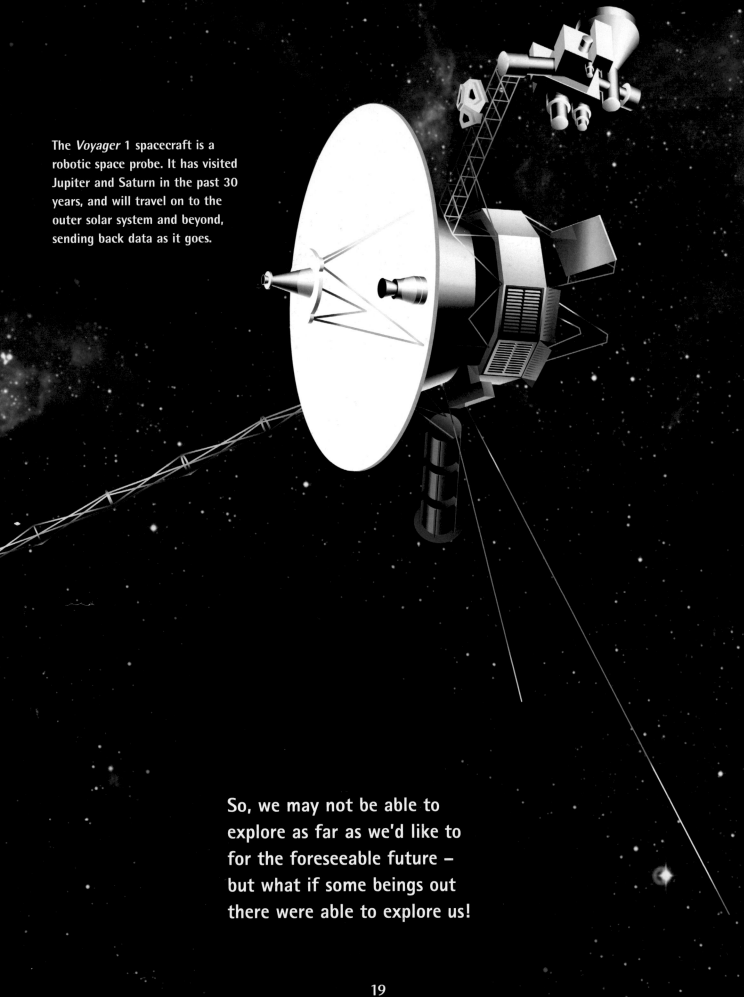

The *Voyager* 1 spacecraft is a robotic space probe. It has visited Jupiter and Saturn in the past 30 years, and will travel on to the outer solar system and beyond, sending back data as it goes.

So, we may not be able to explore as far as we'd like to for the foreseeable future – but what if some beings out there were able to explore us!

Who's out there?

To reach Proxima Centauri by spaceship would take at least 25,000 years, and even if you made the trip you still wouldn't be anywhere except at a lonely clutch of stars in the middle of a vast nowhere.

What else is out there, beyond the solar system? Well, nothing much and a great deal, depending on how you look at it.

An awful lot of nothing much

Nothing is as empty as the emptiness of interstellar space. And there is a great deal of this nothing much until you get to the next bit of something. Our nearest neighbour in the cosmos, Proxima Centauri, is a hundred million times further away than a trip to the Moon, and so it would go on if you tried to star-hop your way across the cosmos. Just reaching the centre of our own galaxy would take far longer than we have existed as beings.

Everything's possible

Space, let me repeat, is enormous. The average distance between stars out there is just over 30 million million kilometres. Of course, it is *possible* that alien beings travel billions of kilometres to amuse themselves by planting crop circles in the English countryside, or frightening the daylights out of some poor guy in a truck on a lonely road in Arizona, but it does seem unlikely. Statistically, the probability that there are other thinking beings out there is good. Nobody knows how many stars there are in the Milky Way – perhaps 100 to 400 billion – and the Milky Way is just one of 140 billion or so other galaxies, many of them even larger than ours.

Dropping in for a visit

In the 1960s, an American professor, Frank Drake, worked out the chances of advanced life existing in the cosmos. According to people like Frank Drake, we may be only one of millions of advanced civilizations. Unfortunately, space being spacious, the average distance between any two of these civilizations is reckoned to be at least 200 light years, which is a great deal more than merely saying it makes it sound.

It means, for a start, that even if these beings know we are here and are somehow able to see us on their screens, they're watching light that left Earth 200 years ago. So they're not seeing you and me. They're watching people in silk stockings and powdered wigs – people who don't know what an atom is, or a gene, and who make their electricity by rubbing a rod of amber with a piece of fur and think that's quite a clever trick.

Frank Drake divided the number of stars in a selected part of the universe
- by the number of stars that are likely to have planetary systems;
- by the number of planetary systems that could theoretically support life;
- by the number on which life, having arisen, might advance to a state of intelligence;
- and so on.

In the Milky Way alone, the number of systems where life might evolve could be somewhere in the millions.

The supernova searcher

Let me introduce you to the Reverend Robert Evans. He watches the sky, but not for aliens. He's a supernova searcher extraordinaire!

When the skies are clear and the Moon is not too bright, this quiet and cheerful man lugs a bulky telescope onto the back sun-deck of his home in the Blue Mountains of Australia, about 80 kilometres west of Sydney, and does an extraordinary thing. He looks deep into the past and finds dying stars.

Galaxies through the letterbox

Bob Evans doesn't have a proper observatory in his back yard, with a sliding domed roof and a mechanized chair, just a crowded storeroom off the kitchen where he keeps his books and papers and his telescope, a white cylinder that is about the size and shape of a household hot-water tank. Between the overhang of the roof and the tops of the eucalyptus trees, he has only a letterbox view of the sky, but he says it's more than good enough for his purposes. Only about 6,000 stars are visible to the naked eye from Earth, and only about 2,000 can be seen from any one spot. But with his 16-inch telescope, Bob Evans can see whole galaxies. In all, he can see between 50,000 and 100,000 galaxies – each containing tens of billions of stars.

Find the grain

To understand how clever Bob Evans is, imagine a dining-room packed with 1,500 tables. Each is covered in a black tablecloth over which a handful of salt has been spilled. The scattered grains can be thought of as a galaxy. Now add one grain of salt to just one table. At a glance Bob Evans will spot it. He'll find his 'odd-man-out' grain – his supernova!

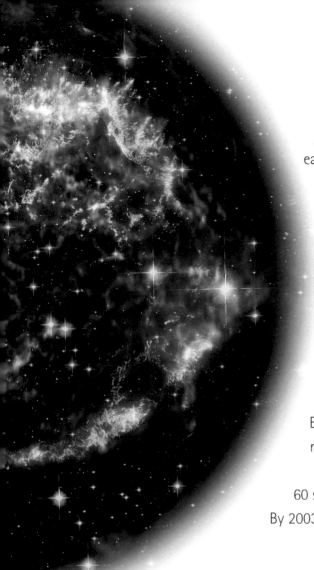

Finding supernovae

Looking into the past is the easy part. Glance at the night sky and what you see is history – lots of it – not the stars as they are now, but as they were when their light left them. Any bright star we can see may have burned out long ago and news of it just hasn't reached us yet. Stars die all the time. Bob Evans tries to spot those last moments. In 1980, before he started looking, fewer than 60 supernovae had been found. By 2003, Evans had found 36 more.

Fritz Zwicky – superstar astronomer

The term 'supernova' was coined in the 1930s by a scientist called Fritz Zwicky. Zwicky was interested in occasional, unexplained points of light that appeared in the sky, new stars. It occurred to him that if a star collapsed, the atoms that formed its core would be crushed together and their electrons forced into the nucleus to form neutrons. This is called a neutron star.

Imagine a million really weighty cannonballs squeezed down to the size of a marble and – well, you're still not even close. The core of a neutron star is so dense that a single spoonful of matter from it would weigh more than 500 billion kilograms. A spoonful! But there was more. Zwicky realized that after the collapse of such a star there would be a huge amount of energy left over – enough to make the biggest bang in the universe.

He called these explosions 'supernovae'.

What if a star exploded nearby?

Our nearest stellar neighbour is Alpha Centauri, a star that is 4.3 light years away. If it exploded, would we have 4.3 years to watch the explosion spreading across the sky, as if tipped from a giant can? Would we have four and a bit years to watch our doom advancing towards us, knowing that when it finally arrived, it would blow the skin right off our bones?

The answer is No!

The news of such an event would travel at the speed of light – so would the destruction, which means we'd see it and die from it in the same instant.

But don't worry – it's not going to happen.

It takes a star ten to twenty times bigger than our Sun to make a supernova, and the nearest possible star of that size is Betelgeuse, which is far too far away. So relax!

Supernovae are extremely rare. In a typical galaxy consisting of 100 billion stars, a supernova will occur on average just once in every 200 or 300 years.

Back on Earth

By the early 1700s, people had become infected with a powerful desire to understand the Earth. Now, two great scientists would come close to finding the answers to some important questions.

Halley did not discover the comet that bears his name. He merely recognized that the comet he saw in 1682 was the same one that had been seen by others in 1456, 1531 and 1607.

A brilliant inventor and scientist . . .

Edmond Halley, the British astronomer, was an exceptional figure. In the course of his long career, Halley was a sea captain, a cartographer, a professor of geometry at the University of Oxford, deputy controller of the Royal Mint, Astronomer Royal, and inventor of the deep-sea diving bell. He wrote on magnetism, tides and the motions of the planets. He invented the weather map and a life-expectancy table, proposed ways of working out the age of the Earth and its distance from the Sun and even came up with a way of keeping fish fresh.

. . . meets a genius

In 1683, Halley and the architect Sir Christopher Wren were dining with colleagues when the conversation turned to the way planets and other bodies moved through space. It was known that planets would normally orbit on a kind of oval path known as an ellipse, but it wasn't understood why. Wren generously offered a prize worth 40 shillings (equal to a couple of weeks' pay) to whichever of his colleagues could provide a solution.

Halley was so keen to win this, he travelled to Cambridge University and boldly called upon a professor of mathematics there, Isaac Newton, in the hope that he'd get some help. Sir Isaac replied immediately that he knew the answer. But Halley couldn't claim his prize money yet. It would be another two years before Newton actually produced his findings in the three-volume *Philosophiae Naturalis Principia Mathematica*, known as the *Principia*.

Oddkin bodkin!

Isaac Newton was a decidedly odd figure – brilliant beyond measure, but solitary, joyless, prickly to the point of paranoia, and capable of the strangest behaviour. He built his own laboratory where he engaged in the most bizarre experiments. Once he inserted a bodkin – a long needle of the sort used for sewing leather – into his eye socket and rubbed it around just to see what would happen. Miraculously, nothing did – at least nothing lasting.

Falling into place

Newton's theories made him instantly famous. Although it has been called 'one of the most inaccessible books ever written', the *Principia* was a beacon to those who could follow it. Amongst other things, it explained the orbits of planets and comets and suchlike, as well as the attractive force that got them moving in the first place – gravity. A couple of brief multiplications, a simple division, and bingo, you know your gravitational position wherever you go.

Newton's formula was the first real universal law of nature. Suddenly every motion in the universe made sense – the slosh and roll of ocean tides, the motions of planets, why cannonballs trace an arc before thudding back to Earth and why we aren't flung into space as the planet spins beneath us at hundreds of miles an hour.

Eventually, Newton came up with what he called the universal law of gravitation. This states that every object in the universe exerts a tug on every other. It may not seem like it, but as you sit here now you are pulling everything around you – walls, ceiling, lamp, pet cat – towards you with your own very little gravitational field. And these things are also pulling on you.

At the heart of Newton's theories were the three laws of motion:

1. A thing moves in the direction in which it is pushed;

2. The thing will keep moving in a straight line at a constant speed until some other force acts to change its speed or direction;

3. Every action has an equal and opposite reaction.

Meanwhile, well before Newton formulated his theories, scientists of all kinds had been trying to work out the size of the Earth.

Measuring the Earth

For half a century, geographers had been using mathematics and a back-breaking technique of stretching heavy chains between two points, known as triangulation.

Triangulation was the method used by a Greek astronomer, Hipparchus of Nicaea, in 150 BC, to work out the Moon's distance from the Earth.

How it works

Triangulation is based on the geometric fact that if you know the length of one side of a triangle and the angles of two corners, you can work out all its other dimensions without leaving your chair. Suppose, by way of example, that you and I decided we wished to know how far it is to the Moon. The first thing we must do is to put some distance between us. So let's say for argument that you stay in Paris and I go to Moscow and we both look at the Moon at the same time.

- Now, if you draw straight lines to connect you and me and the Moon, you will form a triangle.
- Measure the length of the triangle's base line between you and me, and the angles of our two corners.
- Because the interior angles of a triangle always add up to 180 degrees, if you know the sum of two of the angles, you can instantly calculate the third; and knowing the shape of a triangle and the lengths of one side tells you the lengths of the other sides.

angle   angle

base line measurement

Steel chains

In order to measure horizontal distances, the chains or tapes had to be pulled tight since extremes of hot or cold in the temperature would make them sag or shrink. It was also vital that the measuring instrument was kept level.

London to York

One of the first attempts to use triangulation to measure Earth's distances was undertaken by a young English mathematician named Richard Norwood. Norwood, whose first love was trigonometry and thus angles, decided to use triangulation to measure the length of one degree of Earth's meridian, and so calculate the distance round the whole of the planet's circumference.

In 1633, starting with his back against the Tower of London, he spent two devoted years marching 208 miles north to York, repeatedly stretching and measuring a length of chain as he went, all the while making the most meticulous adjustments for the rise and fall of the land and the twists and turns in the road. The final step was to measure the angle of the Sun at York at the same time of day and on the same day of the year as he had made his first measurement in London. It was an ambitious undertaking but, as it turned out, Norwood was accurate to within about 600 yards.

What is a meridian?

A meridian is a north–south line drawn between the North and South Poles and used by astronomers to take measurements. The meridian line that runs through Greenwich, UK, represents Longitude Zero (0°). Every place on the Earth is measured in terms of its angle east or west of this line.

Unfortunately, the task of measuring Earth's size was about to become more complicated...

Earth's bulge

One revelation in Newton's *Principia* became almost immediately controversial. This was the suggestion that the Earth is not quite round.

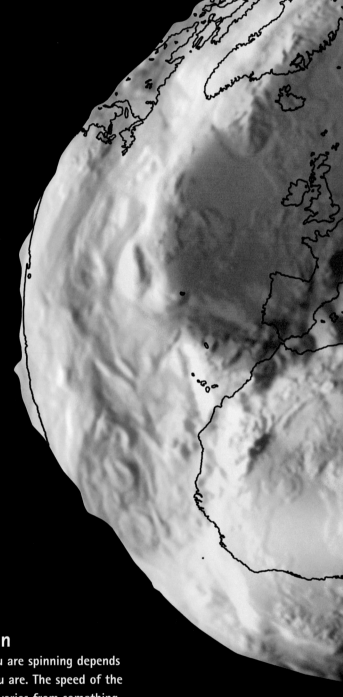

An expanding middle

According to Newton's theory, the centrifugal force of the Earth's spin should result in a slight flattening at the Poles and a bulging at the Equator, which would make the planet slightly squashed.

That meant that the length of a degree of meridian would shorten as you moved away from the Poles. This was not good news for those people whose measurements of the planets were based on the assumption that it was a perfect sphere.

Your spin

How fast you are spinning depends on where you are. The speed of the Earth's spin varies from something about 1,700 kilometres an hour at the Equator, to zero at the poles. In London, for example, the speed is 1,046 kilometres an hour.

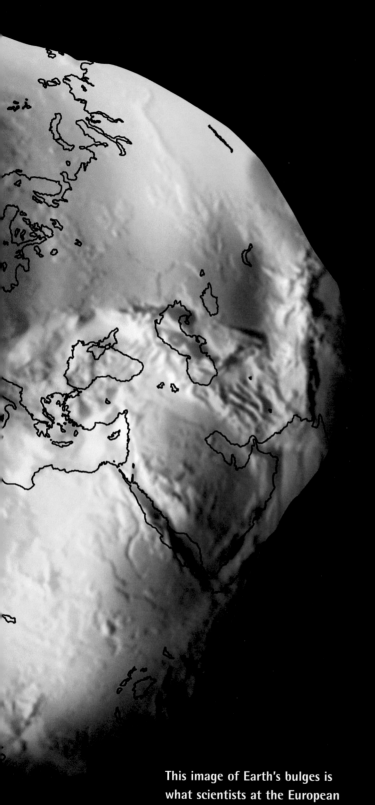

The shape of Earth

Data from satellites taken over the past ten years show that the bulge in the Earth's physical shape at the Equator is growing. This is all to do with changes in Earth's gravity field.

Scientists believe that the oceans may be the reason behind this. As the climate changes, large areas of ice are melting and filling the oceans with colder water. This is happening particularly around the oceans of the Antarctic, and the Pacific and Indian Oceans.

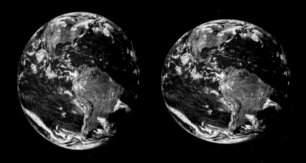

The result is that the Earth is starting to look more like a rugby ball than a soccer ball. Although the changes have taken place over tens of thousands of years, it is only now, using sophisticated NASA satellites, that these changes can be tracked.

This image of Earth's bulges is what scientists at the European Space Agency are expecting to see once their new survey satellite is launched.

Back in the early 1700s, Newton's bulge theory would spur those who believed in it – as well as those who didn't – to fresh measuring endeavours all over the planet.

How far round?

One of the least cheerful and friendly scientific field trips of all time was the French expedition to Peru in 1735. It was led by a mathematician named Pierre Bouguer and a soldier-explorer called Charles Marie de La Condamine, and involved a party of scientists and adventurers whose mission it was to measure distances through the Andes.

Circumference matters

The French party's goal was to help settle the question of the circumference of the planet. The party would measure along a line reaching from Yarouqui, near Quito, to just beyond Cuenca in what is now Ecuador – a distance of about 200 mountainous miles – and this would tell them all they wanted to know.

Almost at once things began to go wrong. In Quito, the visitors somehow angered the locals and were chased out of town by a mob armed with stones. Soon afterwards, the expedition's doctor was murdered in a misunderstanding over a woman.

The botanist went mad. Others died of fevers and falls. The third most senior member of the party ran off with a young girl and couldn't be persuaded to return. At one point, the group had to stop work for eight months while La Condamine rode off to Lima to sort out a problem with their permits. Eventually, he and Bouguer stopped speaking and refused to work together.

Everywhere the dwindling party went it was met with the deepest suspicion from officials who found it difficult to believe that a group of French scientists would travel halfway around the world in order to measure it. It made no sense at all.

High in the Andes

Two and a half centuries later, it still seems a reasonable question. Why didn't the French take their measurements in France and save themselves all the bother of their Andean adventure?

Well, they chose the Andes because they needed to measure near the Equator and establish if Newton had been right – that there was indeed a bulge in the planet there; also because they reasoned that mountains would give them good sightlines. In fact, the Andes were so constantly lost in cloud that the team often had to wait weeks for an hour's clear surveying. On top of that, not only did they have to scale some of the world's most challenging mountains – that defeated even their mules – but to reach them in the first place, they had to ford wild rivers, hack their way through jungles, and cross miles of high, stony desert, nearly all of it unmapped and far from any source of supplies.

But Bouguer and La Condamine were nothing if not tenacious, and they stuck to the task for nine and a half long, grim, sun-blistered years.

Shortly before concluding the project, word reached them that a second French team, taking measurements in northern Scandinavia (and facing notable discomforts of their own, from squelching bogs to dangerous ice floes), had found that the Earth wasn't exactly round, just as Newton had promised.

The Earth was 27 miles fatter when measured round the Equator than when measured from top to bottom around the Poles.

Bouguer and La Condamine had spent nearly a decade working towards a result they didn't wish to find, only to learn that they weren't even the first to find it. Feeling down at heart, they completed their survey. Then, still not speaking, they returned to the coast and took separate ships back home.

Tracking Venus

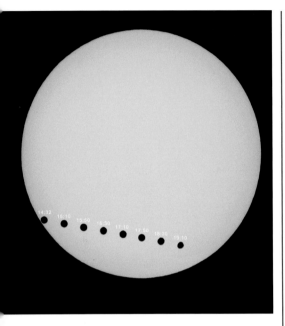

This photo tracks the path of Venus at intervals as it moves across the face of the Sun. The entire transit takes just over three hours.

Transits of Venus don't occur regularly. They come in pairs eight years apart, but then don't happen for a century or more.

It was Edmond Halley who suggested that if you measured the passage of the planet Venus across the face of the Sun from selected points on the Earth, you could use the principles of triangulation to work out the distance from the Earth to the Sun. From there, you would also be able to measure the distances to all the other bodies in the solar system.

From all around the globe

So, when the next transit fell due in 1761, nearly two decades after Halley's death, the scientific world was more ready than it ever had been for an astronomical event before. With an instinct for hardship and suffering that was typical of the age, scientists set off for more than a hundred locations around the globe – to Siberia, China, South Africa, Indonesia and the woods of Wisconsin, USA, among many others. France dispatched 32 observers, Britain 18 more, and still others set out from Sweden, Russia, Italy, Germany, Ireland and elsewhere.

An ill-fated quest

It was history's first co-operative, international scientific venture and almost everywhere it ran into problems. Many observers were waylaid by war, sickness or shipwreck. Others made it to their destinations but opened their crates to find equipment broken or warped by tropical heat. A Frenchman, Jean Chappe, spent months travelling to Siberia by coach, boat and sleigh, nursing his delicate instruments over every perilous bump, only to find the last vital stretch blocked by swollen rivers, the result of unusually heavy spring rains, which the locals were swift to blame on him after they saw him pointing strange instruments at the sky.

Twice unlucky

Unluckier still was Guillaume Le Gentil, who set off from France a year ahead of time to observe the transit from India. Sadly, various setbacks left him still at sea on the day of the transit – just about the worst place to be, since steady measurements were impossible on a pitching ship. Undaunted, Le Gentil continued on to India to await the next transit in 1769. With eight years to prepare, he erected a first-rate viewing station, tested and re-tested his instruments and had everything in a state of perfect readiness. On the morning of the second transit, 4 June 1769, he awoke to a fine day; but, just as Venus began its pass, a cloud slid in front of the Sun and remained there for almost exactly the duration of the transit of three hours, fourteen minutes and seven seconds.

Joseph Lalande

The Venus transit expedition of 1761 may have been a total disaster but on the return of the various scientists from the 1769 one, there was enough information for the French astronomer Joseph Lalande to calculate that the average distance from the Earth to the Sun was a little over 93 million miles. Two further transits in the 1800s allowed astronomers to put the figure at 92.95 million miles. The precise distance, we now know, is 92.96 million miles, or 149.57 million kilometres.

In the end, the successful charting of a Venus transit fell to a little-known English sea captain named James Cook. He watched the later 1769 transit from an observatory set up on the island of Tahiti. (He then went on to chart and claim Australia for the British crown.)

The painstaking measurements taken by these scientists meant that the Earth at last had a position in space.

33

Weighing the Earth

Newton had suggested that if you hung a weighted plumb-line near a mountain, it would lean very slightly towards it, pulled by the mountain's gravitational mass as well as by the Earth's. If you then measured the amount of pull and worked out the mountain's weight – strictly speaking, its mass – you could calculate the basic value of gravity – and, along with it, the weight or mass of the Earth.

Maskelyne's mountain

Nevil Maskelyne, the British Astronomer Royal, was one of many who took up Newton's challenge to measure the true weight of Earth. He knew he needed to find a mountain with a regular, near symmetrical shape in order to carry out his experiments. A British organization, the Royal Society, agreed to engage a reliable figure to tour the British Isles to see if such a mountain could be found and they appointed the astronomer and surveyor Charles Mason. Mason found a mountain for the gravitational deflection experiment. It was in Scotland and was called Schiehallion.

Mason and Dixon

Charles Mason and his fellow scientist Jeremiah Dixon had travelled to Sumatra to chart the Venus transit. Like many on this ill-fated venture, they hadn't even got there! A year later, they'd set off to survey their way through dangerous American wilderness to settle a boundary dispute between Pennsylvania and Maryland. The result was the famous Mason–Dixon line, which later became the dividing line between the slave and free states.

Back to Maskelyne

Since Mason announced he was too busy to do the measuring work himself, the job fell to Maskelyne. So, for four months in the summer of 1774, the Astronomer Royal lived in a tent in a remote Scottish glen and spent his days directing a team of surveyors, who took hundreds of measurements from every possible position.

To find the mass of the mountain from all these numbers required a great deal of tedious calculating, for which a geologist named Charles Hutton was engaged. The surveyors had soon covered a map with scores of figures, each marking a height at some point on or around the mountain. It was essentially just a confusing mass of numbers.

Charles Hutton

Hutton noticed that if he used a pencil to connect points of equal height, it all became much more orderly. Indeed, one could instantly get a sense of the overall shape and slope of the mountain. He'd used contour lines. From his measurements, Hutton calculated the mass of the Earth at the equivalent of 4,536 million million metric tonnes.

From this he then went on to work out the masses of all the other major bodies in the solar system, including the Sun. So from this one experiment we learned the weights of the Earth, the Sun, the Moon, the other planets and their moons, and got contour lines into the bargain – not bad for a summer's work.

Featherweight measures

Not everyone was satisfied with the Schiehallion experiment, however. It seemed it wasn't possible to get a truly accurate figure without knowing the actual density, or solidity, of the mountain.

When assembled, Michell's apparatus looked like an eighteenth-century version of the kind of weight-training machine you find in a gym. It incorporated weights, shafts, counterweights, pendulums and torsion wires. At the heart of the machine were two 350-pound lead balls.

John Michell

One improbable person who turned his mind to the matter was a country parson named John Michell. Despite his humble situation, Michell was one of the great scientific thinkers of the 1700s. He discovered the wave-like nature of earthquakes, made telescopes, and, quite extraordinarily, worked out the existence of black holes 200 years before anyone else – a leap that not even Newton could make. But of everything that Michell accomplished, nothing was more ingenious or had greater impact than a machine he designed and built for measuring the weight of the Earth.

The idea behind Michell's machine was to measure how gravity affects the way an object will collide and bounce against a flat surface. From this would come the first measurement of the mysterious force known as the gravitational constant, from which the mass of the Earth could be estimated.

Henry Cavendish

Unfortunately, John Michell died before he could conduct the experiments which would accurately weigh Earth, and both the idea and the equipment were passed to a brilliant, but amazingly shy, London scientist named Henry Cavendish. Cavendish was born into a life of privilege – his grandfathers were the dukes of Devonshire and Kent. He was the most gifted English scientist of his age, but also the strangest. He was so shy that visitors were not welcome and even his housekeeper had to communicate with him by letter.

A delicate measure

In the late summer of 1797, Cavendish turned his attention to the crates of equipment that had been left to him by John Michell. Cavendish was now trying to measure gravity at a featherweight level. Delicacy was the keyword. Not a whisper of disturbance could be allowed into the room containing Michell's apparatus, so Cavendish took up a position in an adjoining room and made his observations with a telescope aimed through a peephole. The work was incredibly exacting, involving 17 delicate, interconnected measurements, which together took nearly a year to complete. When at last he had finished his calculations, Cavendish announced that the Earth weighed a little over six billion trillion metric tonnes. Interestingly, all of this merely confirmed estimates Newton made 110 years earlier without conducting any experiments at all.

Best guess

Today, scientists have at their disposal machines so precise they can detect the weight of a single bacterium, and so sensitive that readings can be disturbed by someone yawning 20 metres away, but they have not significantly improved on Cavendish's measurements of 1797.

Gentle gravity

Because gravity holds planets in orbit and makes falling objects land with a bang, we tend to think of it as a powerful force, but it isn't really. It's only powerful in a kind of collective sense, when one massive object, like the Sun, holds onto another massive object, like Earth. In itself, gravity is extraordinarily weak. Each time you pick up a book from a table or a coin from the floor, you effortlessly overcome the force of gravity of an entire planet.

The current best estimate for the Earth's weight is 5.9725 billion trillion tonnes, a difference of only about 1 per cent from Cavendish's finding.

So, here we are . . .

What we know so far:

- We know about the Big Bang;
- about the solar system;
- about how supernovae form and explode;
- about gravity;
- about using triangulation to measure distances and angles;
- about Pluto's lost moon;
- about cosmic radiation;
- . . . and a whole lot more.

We have a universe and a planet, and a great deal of guesswork that's slowly turning into hard fact about how big Earth is, how round, how heavy and how far from its neighbours in the solar system it is. In short, we've already learned a lot.

How long is Earth's circumference?

1637 Richard Norwood uses a method of measuring involving triangles, known as triangulation, and comes up with a result that's close – but not quite there.

1684 Edmond Halley, investigating the movement of the planets, is clever enough to enlist the help of the brilliant Isaac Newton.

1687 Isaac Newton comes to grips with gravity and the three laws of motion in his famous work, the *Principia*, and Halley makes sure this gets published.

1735 Pierre Bouguer and Charles Marie de La Condamine try to measure the length of one degree of meridian (on their way to working out Earth's circumference) by climbing up and down the Andes in South America.

1736 A second French team confirms that the Earth bulges around the Equator.

38

How far is Earth from the Sun?

1761 Following the advice of Edmond Halley (who is long since dead), scientists from all over the world go rushing off to far-flung places to observe the Venus transit and try to use it as a means of measuring the distance of Earth from the Sun.

How much does Earth weigh?

1774 Nevil Maskelyne decides to use Isaac Newton's idea for measuring the weight of Earth involving gravity – and yet more triangulation and mountain climbing. Maskelyne climbs Schiehallion in Scotland, along with mathematician Charles Hutton. Hutton invents contour lines while he's doing the maths, and now declares that Earth weighs nearly 5,000 million million metric tonnes.

1793 John Michell leaves behind a design for a machine that will accurately weigh the Earth.

1797 Henry Cavendish uses Michell's machine to weigh in Earth at six billion trillion metric tonnes. He's just 1 per cent out or so – not bad!

So, now let's find out what our Earth is made up of and just how long it's been around.

Finding Earth's age

By the late 1700s, scientists knew very precisely the shape and dimensions of the Earth, its distance from the Sun and planets, and its weight. So you might think that working out its age would be relatively straightforward. But no! Human beings would split the atom and invent television, nylon and instant coffee before they would figure out the age of their own planet.

Water erosion is a powerful force in carving out rock and carrying it away.

Mountain-climbing shells

Among the questions that attracted interest was one that had puzzled people for a very long time – namely, why ancient clam shells and other marine fossils were so often found on mountaintops.
How on earth did they get there?

It was left to a brilliant Scottish scientist, James Hutton, to suggest an answer. From looking at his own farmland, he could see that soil was created by the erosion of rocks. Particles of this soil were continually washed away and carried off by streams and rivers to be deposited elsewhere. He realized that if such a process were carried to its natural conclusion, then the Earth would eventually be worn quite smooth. Yet everywhere around him there were hills.

Clearly, there had to be something else going on that created new hills and mountains and kept the cycle going. The marine fossils on mountaintops, Hutton decided, had not been deposited during floods, but had risen along with the mountains themselves.

Neptune versus Pluto

One group of scientists, known as the Neptunists, were convinced that everything on the Earth, including sea shells found in impossibly lofty places, could be explained by rising and falling sea levels. They believed that mountains, hills and other features were as old as the Earth itself, and were changed only when water sloshed over them during periods of global flooding.

Opposing them were the Plutonists, who claimed that volcanoes and earthquakes continually changed the face of the planet and that this owed nothing to over-energetic seas. The Plutonists also raised awkward questions about where all the water would have gone when it wasn't in flood. If there had been enough of it at times to cover the Alps, then where did it go the rest of the time? They believed, rightly, that the Earth was subject to huge internal forces as well as surface ones. However, they still couldn't explain how all those clam shells got up the mountain.

A heaving Earth

Hutton also worked out that it was heat within the Earth that created new rocks and continents and thrust up mountain chains. (Geologists wouldn't grasp the full implications of this thought until 200 years later, when they finally adopted the concept of plate tectonics.) Above all, what Hutton's theories suggested was that the processes that shaped Earth required huge amounts of time.
Earth was far older than anyone had ever dreamed.

A new science

It would take another hundred years or so before science could finally tackle the question of how old Earth was. Hutton had been brilliant but he'd found it impossible to set down his ideas in a way that anyone could understand. It was left to those who took over his papers to explain the genius behind his work and to lead the way to the birth of a new science – geology.

Geology – the study of rocks, soil and all the materials that make up our planet, and how they formed and changed – all this would transform our entire understanding of the Earth.

The stone-breakers

In the winter of 1807, like-minded men got together at the Freemasons Tavern at Long Acre, Covent Garden, in London, UK, to form a dining club which they called, rather grandly, the Geological Society.

The idea was to meet once a month to swap geological ideas over a hearty dinner. The price of the meal was set at a deliberately hefty 15 shillings. These weren't people with a financial interest in rocks and minerals, or even academics for the most part, but simply gentlemen with the wealth and time to indulge a hobby at a more or less professional level. It was taken seriously and they tended to dress with appropriate gravity, in suits and top hats. In barely a decade, membership grew to 400 – still all gentlemen, of course – and the Geological Society was emerging as the top scientific society in the country. By 1830 there were 745 of these eager geologists, and the world would never see their like again.

The dinners stopped each June, when virtually all of the members went off to spend the summer doing fieldwork. Throughout the modern, thinking world, but especially in Britain, men of learning ventured into the countryside to do a little 'stone-breaking', as they called it.

Charles Lyell

Reverend William Buckland

Charles Lyell would become the most famous of the group. His father was a leading authority on mosses. From him, Lyell gained an interest in natural history, and later, having fallen under the spell of William Buckland, joined his new colleague on a scientific trip to Scotland and devoted himself entirely to geology.

Reverend William Buckland of Oxford is fondly remembered for his eccentric behaviour. He had a menagerie of wild animals, some large and dangerous, which were allowed to wander through his house and garden. He also tried to eat his way through every animal in creation. Depending on whim and availability, guests to Buckland's house might be served baked guinea pig, mice in batter, roasted hedgehog or boiled Southeast Asian sea slug. He became the leading authority on coprolites – fossilized faeces – and had a table made entirely out of specimens.

Dr James Parkinson

Roderick Murchison

Dr James Parkinson was involved in a mad conspiracy called 'the Pop-gun Plot'. The plan was to shoot the English King, George III, in the neck with a poisoned dart. Parkinson was arrested and almost got sent to Australia. However, once he'd calmed down, he developed an interest in geology, and became one of the founding members of the Geological Society.

Roderick Murchison spent the first 30 or so years of his life galloping after foxes and turning birds into puffs of drifting feathers with buckshot. Then he suddenly discovered an interest in rocks and became, with astounding speed, a giant of geological science.

Slow and steady does it

In the early 1800s, there arose a new and long-running argument amongst geologists as to how speedily the events that shaped Earth had happened. This took over from the old argument about Neptune and Pluto, but more importantly it allowed Lyell to emerge as the father of modern geological thought.

The Catastrophists

This group, as you might expect from the name, believed that the Earth was shaped by short, sharp, cataclysmic events – floods, principally, which is why catastrophism and Neptunism are often bundled together. Catastrophists believed that extinctions were part of a series of dramatic events in which animals were repeatedly wiped out and replaced with new sets.

The Uniformitarians

This group, by contrast, believed that changes on Earth were gradual and happened slowly, over immense spans of time. Hutton was really the father of this theory and a scientist without rival when it came to understanding the mysterious slow processes that shaped the Earth. But Lyell was the one most people read and certainly the easier of the two men to comprehend, so inevitably he was the one who got all the glory.

A man of influence

Lyell was a university professor of geology in London when he produced *The Principles of Geology*. In this he set out his belief that the Earth's shifts were uniform and steady – that everything that had ever happened in the past could be explained by events still going on today. It's nearly impossible to overstate his influence. *The Principles of Geology* shaped geological thinking far into the twentieth century.

Just like Hutton before him, Lyell was paving the way for the discovery of something which we're all familiar with today – tectonic plates. Soon scientists would understand that the Earth's crust wasn't a solid skin, but a whole series of 'pieces of skin' – what are commonly known as continental plates. Each of these is moving and shifting – albeit very, very slowly – across the liquid magma below. And as they shift, they collide and squeeze against each other, causing great shifts in the landscape and forming vast mountain chains and valleys. As useful as this discovery was, it still didn't put a date on the age of Earth – although it was clearly going to be a good deal older than most people had thought.

Lyell rejected the notion that animals and plants could suddenly be wiped out, and believed that all the main animal groups – mammals, reptiles, fish and so on – had co-existed since the dawn of time. On all this he would be proved wrong.

Not perfect though!

Lyell's oversights were not inconsiderable. He failed to explain convincingly how mountain ranges were formed, and overlooked glaciers as an agent of change. He refused to accept the idea of ice ages and was confident that mammals had been on the planet as long as plants or fish.

Geologists continued to place rocks and fossils in order by age, although they had no idea how long any of those ages were.

Finding fossils

William Smith's unique map, showing the geology of England, Wales and part of Scotland, helped industrialists locate coal- and mineral-bearing rocks where they could set up mines and factories. This helped Britain become a leader in world manufacturing.

The Englishman William Smith was a young construction supervisor on the Somerset Coal Canal. On the evening of 5 January 1796, he was sitting in a coaching inn when he jotted down the notion that would eventually make his reputation.

Mapping the rocks

Smith knew that to interpret rocks, there needed to be some means of telling whether rocks dating from one period and found in one part of the country were younger or older than rocks from a different period which had been found in another area.

At every change in the rock strata, or layers, certain species of fossil disappeared while others continued to be found at higher levels. By noting which species appeared in which strata, Smith believed you could work out the relative ages of rocks. Drawing on his knowledge as a surveyor, he began to make a map of Britain's rock strata, which, in time, became the basis of modern geology.

The answer to dating rocks lay with fossils.

Fossil of an Early Permian reptile.

A clever collector

In 1812, at Lyme Regis, a small town on the south coast of England, an extraordinary child named Mary Anning found a strange fossilized sea monster, now known as an ichthyosaur. It was five metres long and embedded in steep and dangerous cliffs along the coast.

It was the start of a remarkable career. Anning would spend the next 35 years gathering fossils. She would find the first plesiosaur, another marine monster, and one of the first and best pterodactyls.

It wasn't simply that Anning was good at spotting fossils – but that she could extract them with the greatest delicacy and without damaging them. At the Natural History Museum in London, you can appreciate the scale and beauty of what this young woman achieved, working virtually unaided and with the most basic tools. Although untrained, Anning was also able to provide competent drawings and descriptions for scholars.

This ammonite fossil is 150 million years old. Ammonites are an extinct group of marine animals. They are called index fossils because it is often possible to link the rock layer in which they are found to specific geological time periods.

Dinosaur bones trapped in layers of hillside rock.

The plesiosaurus took Mary Anning ten years of patient excavation.

Dating the rocks

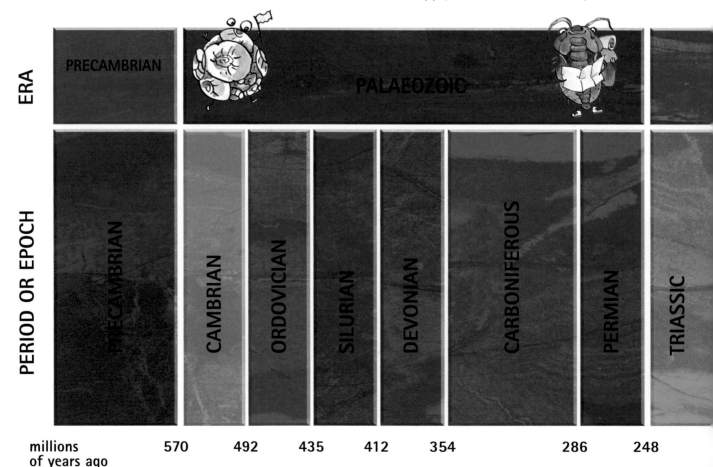

CENOZOIC

MESOZOIC

PALAEOZOIC

PRECAMBRIAN

Rock layers are dated by the period in which they formed.

It's hard to imagine now, but geology gripped the nineteenth century in a way that no science ever had or would do again. Much of this was to do with William Smith and Charles Lyell, who delighted in ordering things on maps and charts.

Nowadays, geological time is broadly divided into four great chunks known as eras: Precambrian, Palaeozoic (from the Greek meaning 'old life'), Mesozoic ('middle life') and Cenozoic ('recent life'). These four eras are further divided into a dozen or so sub-groups, usually called periods. Most of these are reasonably well known: Cretaceous, Jurassic, Triassic, Silurian, and so on. It was Lyell who introduced the Pleistocene, Miocene, etc. – which apply to the last 65 million years.

ERA	PRECAMBRIAN	PALAEOZOIC						
PERIOD OR EPOCH	PRECAMBRIAN	CAMBRIAN	ORDOVICIAN	SILURIAN	DEVONIAN	CARBONIFEROUS	PERMIAN	TRIASSIC

millions of years ago   570   492   435   412   354   286   248

It's mine!

Geology had a great deal of sorting out to do, and not all of it went smoothly. From the outset, geologists tried to categorize rocks by the periods in which they were laid down, but there were often bitter disagreements about where to put the dividing lines.

One major argument arose when an English geologist, the Reverend Adam Sedgwick, claimed for the Cambrian period a layer of rock that Roderick Murchison (an early member of the British Geological Society, if you remember) believed belonged rightly to the Silurian. The dispute raged for years and grew extremely heated. However, the fight was finally settled in 1879 with the simple solution of coming up with a new period, the Ordovician, which was neatly inserted between the Cambrian and Silurian.

Geological calendar

There will be no testing here, but if you are ever required to memorize the geological terms for some exam, you might wish to remember this piece of helpful advice. Think of the eras (Precambrian, Palaeozoic, Mesozoic and Cenozoic) as seasons in a year and the periods (Permian, Triassic, Jurassic, etc.) as the months.

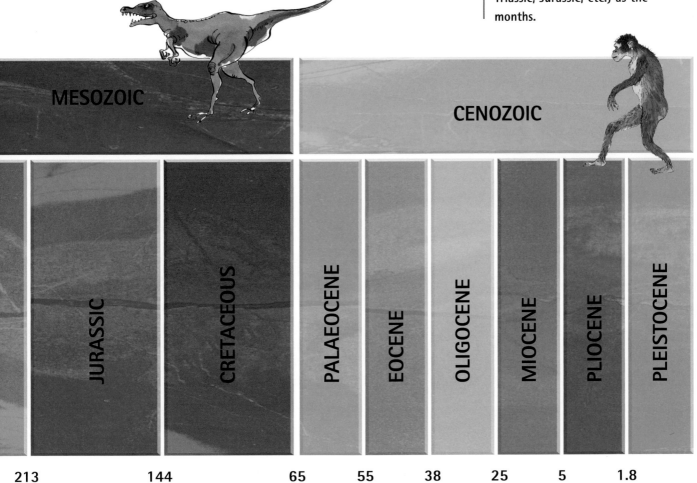

MESOZOIC

CENOZOIC

JURASSIC

CRETACEOUS

PALAEOCENE

EOCENE

OLIGOCENE

MIOCENE

PLIOCENE

PLEISTOCENE

213   144   65   55   38   25   5   1.8

Tooth and claw

There was now plenty of fossil evidence to help the rock-daters. As far back as 1787, someone in New Jersey, USA, had found an enormous thigh bone sticking out of a stream bank at a place called Woodbury Creek. The bone clearly didn't belong to any species of creature still alive, at least not in New Jersey.

A whopper!

It's now thought to have belonged to a hadrosaur, a large duck-billed dinosaur. At the time, dinosaurs were unknown. The bone was sent to Dr Caspar Wistar, the nation's leading expert in anatomy, who completely failed to recognize its significance and merely made a few cautious and uninspired remarks to the effect that it was indeed a whopper. He therefore missed the chance, half a century ahead of anyone else, to be the discoverer of dinosaurs. Indeed, the bone excited so little interest that it was put in a storeroom and eventually disappeared altogether. So the first dinosaur bone ever found was also the first to be lost.

Challenging America

That the bone didn't attract greater interest is more than a little puzzling, for its appearance came at a time when America was in a froth of excitement about the remains of large, ancient animals. The cause of this was a controversial statement by the great French naturalist the Comte de Buffon that living things in America were inferior in nearly every way to those elsewhere. America, Buffon wrote, was a land of stagnant water, dead soil and small, weak animals, the result of the 'noxious vapours' that rose from its rotting swamps and sunless forests.

We'll show you!

Not surprisingly, such comments didn't go down at all well in America. A troop of twenty soldiers was immediately ordered to go into the northern woods to find a bull moose to present to Buffon as proof of the size and majesty of American quadrupeds. It took the men two weeks to track down a suitable subject. The moose, when shot, unfortunately lacked the imposing horns needed to convince Buffon, but the soldiers thoughtfully included a rack of antlers from an elk or stag with the suggestion that these be attached instead. Who in France, after all, would know?

Discovery at Big Bone Lick

Meanwhile, in Philadelphia, naturalists had begun to assemble the bones of a giant elephant-like creature, later identified, not quite correctly, as a mammoth. The first of these bones had been discovered at a place called Big Bone Lick in Kentucky, but soon others were turning up all over the States. In their keenness to demonstrate the unknown animal's bulk and ferocity, the American naturalists appear to have got slightly carried away. They over-estimated its size by six times and gave it frightening claws, which, in fact, came from a quite different animal altogether – a megalonyx, or giant ground sloth.

Nipple-teeth

In 1795, a selection of these bones made their way to Paris, where they were examined by a rising star in prehistoric studies, known as palaeontology. The young Georges Cuvier was already dazzling people with his genius for taking heaps of random bones and whipping them into a presentable animal form. Realizing that no one in America had written a formal description of this new lumbering beast, Cuvier did so, and became the official discoverer of the mastodon, which means 'nipple-teeth'.

Inventing animals

When tusks were discovered, they were often forced into the animal's head in any number of inventive ways. One restorer screwed the tusks in upside down, like the fangs of a sabre-toothed cat. Another arranged the tusks so that they curved backwards, using the amusing theory that the creature had been aquatic and had used them to anchor itself to trees while dozing.

Bones and more bones

At the same time as William Smith was drawing attention to fossils in England, bones were turning up all over the place. Several times over, various Americans had an opportunity to claim the discovery of dinosaurs for themselves, but these were wasted. For example, in 1806, an expedition from the east to the west of America led by Meriwether Lewis and William Clark passed through the Hell Creek Formation in Montana, an area where fossil hunters would later literally trip over dinosaur bones. The two even examined what was clearly a dinosaur bone embedded in rock, but failed to make anything of it.

Other bones and fossilized footprints were found in a river valley in New England after a farm boy named Plinus Moody spied ancient tracks on a rock ledge. Some of these bones survive, notably those of a small lizard-like dinosaur, the anchisaurus. Found in 1818, they were America's first dinosaur bones to be examined and saved.

By the 1880s extinct creatures of any kind had become the rage.

Dinosaur hunters

In south London, at a place called Crystal Palace Park, there stands a strange and forgotten sight: the world's first life-sized models of dinosaurs. When these models were placed there in 1851, the science of dinosaur hunting had only just begun, and a few key men still had some way to go before we would know as much about these prehistoric creatures as we do today.

Crystal Palace Park was once one of the most popular attractions in London. Quite a lot about the models is not strictly correct. For example, there's an iguanodon whose thumb has been placed on its nose, as a kind of spike, and it stands on four sturdy legs – and not two as it should – looking like a rather stout and awkward dog.

Terrible lizard

Richard Owen is remembered as the man who coined the term 'dinosauria' in 1841. It means 'terrible lizards' and was a curiously inapt name. Dinosaurs, as we now know, weren't all terrible – some were no bigger than rabbits and probably extremely shy – and the one thing they most certainly were not was lizards. Owen was aware that the creatures were reptiles, but for some reason chose not to use the correct Greek word.

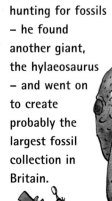

A model dinosaur is given its annual scrub at the Crystal Palace Park in south London, UK, 1927.

The first iguanodon

Gideon Algernon Mantell was a country doctor living in Sussex, England. When his wife found a strange stone, Mantell could tell at once it was a fossilized tooth, and after a little study, identified it as a plant-eating reptile, extremely large and from the Cretaceous period. He was right on all counts. Mantell's creature became the iguanodon, named after a basking tropical lizard – which was actually no relation. Mantell continued hunting for fossils – he found another giant, the hylaeosaurus – and went on to create probably the largest fossil collection in Britain.

Fossil feud

Edward Cope and Othniel Charles Marsh were fossil hunters who changed the world of palaeontology. They started out as friends, even naming fossil species after each other, but ended up as bitter enemies. However, over the years, the two men between them increased the number of known dinosaur species in America from nine to almost 150. Nearly every dinosaur that the average person can name – stegosaurus, brontosaurus, diplodocus, triceratops – was found by one or other of them.

This huge model of a megalosaurus stands in Crystal Palace Park.

It's bone time

Some wild guesses!

In 1650, Archbishop James Ussher of the Church of Ireland made a careful study of the Bible and concluded that the Earth had been created at midday on 23 October 4004 BC.

When William Buckland tried to put a date on an ichthyosaurus skeleton, he could only suggest that it had lived somewhere between 'ten thousand and more than ten thousand times ten thousand years ago'.

The Scotsman William Thomson, Lord Kelvin, first suggested Earth was 98 million years old. Over time, he changed his estimate to a cautious 'between 20 and 400 million years', then proceeded downwards to 100, then to 50, and finally to a mere 24 million years.

At least today we can bring some sophisticated dating techniques to the table. But for most of the 1800s, geologists could draw on nothing more than the most hopeful guesswork.

Guessing game

By the middle of the 1800s, most learned people thought the Earth was at least a few million years old – perhaps tens of millions of years, or even more. However, such was the confusion that by the end of the century, depending on which text you consulted, you could learn that the number of years that stood between us and the first fossil of the Cambrian period was 3 million, 18 million, 600 million, 794 million, or 2.4 billion – or some other number within that range.

A precise age

In 1859, the English biologist Charles Darwin calculated that the geological processes that had created an area of southern England had taken precisely 306,662,400 years to complete. This was remarkably specific; even so, very few people were prepared to believe him since it went against the religious teachings of the time.

Bone Cabin Quarry

In 1898, a trove greater by far than anything found before was discovered at a place called Bone Cabin Quarry in Wyoming, USA. There, hundreds and hundreds of fossil bones were found weathering out on the hills. They were so numerous, in fact, that someone had built a cabin out of them – hence the name. In just the first two seasons of collecting, 45,000 kilos of ancient bones were excavated from the site in the quarry, and tens of thousands more arrived in each of the half-dozen years that followed.

Excavations at Bone Cabin Quarry.

Loads of bones

The upshot is that palaeontologists had literally tonnes of old bones to pick over. The problem was that they still didn't have any idea how old any of these bones were. Worse, the agreed ages for the Earth couldn't comfortably support the number of ages and epochs that the past obviously contained.

Geologists clearly needed help if Earth was ever going to be given an accurate age. This would come from the findings of a new science – it was time for chemistry to take a hand.

The mighty atom

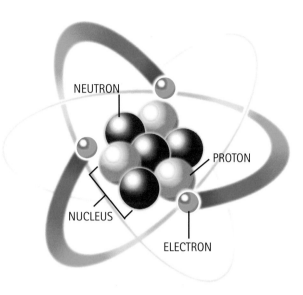

NEUTRON
PROTON
NUCLEUS
ELECTRON

The basis of chemistry is the atom, the matter from which all things are made. Atoms are everywhere and everything is made of them. Even though it would take the great scientist Einstein to prove once and for all that the atom existed, neither the idea of atoms nor the term itself was exactly new. Both had been developed by the ancient Greeks and investigated by many earlier scientists.

The atom

Every atom is made from three kinds of particle:

- **protons, which have a positive electrical charge;**
- **electrons, which have a negative electrical charge;**
- **and neutrons, which have no charge.**

Protons and neutrons are packed into the centre, or nucleus, of the atom while electrons spin around the outside.

Just which one billion of Shakespeare's atoms might you have?

Numbers beyond belief

Atoms are present in numbers that you really cannot conceive. At sea level, at freezing point, one cubic centimetre of air – a space about the size of a sugar cube – will contain 27 million billion molecules. (A molecule is simply two or more atoms working together.) Think how many cubic centimetres it would take to make a universe!

A teeny bit of Shakespeare

Not only do atoms live a very long time, they really get around. Every atom in your body has almost certainly passed through several stars and been part of millions of organisms on its way to becoming you. We each contain so many atoms and are so completely recycled at death that a significant number of our atoms – up to a billion for each of us – probably once belonged to Shakespeare. A billion more may have come from Buddha and Genghis Khan and Beethoven, and any other historical figure you care to name.

When we die, our atoms will break up and move off to find new uses elsewhere – as part of a leaf or drop of dew, or even another human being. Atoms go on practically for ever. Nobody actually knows how long an atom can survive, but it's probably billions of years.

Weighing the atom

The realization that atoms are three things – small, numerous and practically indestructible – and that all things are made from them, was taken up by an Englishman named John Dalton. Dalton was born in 1766. He was so exceptionally bright that at the young age of 12 he was put in charge of the local Quaker school. (We know from his diaries that at about this time he was reading Newton's *Principia* – in the original Latin.) Still in his 20s, he was one of the earliest scientists to suggest that all matter was made up of exceedingly tiny particles, or atoms. But his main contribution was to consider the relative sizes and characters of these atoms and how they fit together.

The lightness scale

Dalton knew, for instance, that hydrogen was the lightest element, so he gave it what he called 'an atomic weight' of 1. He believed also that water consisted of seven parts of oxygen to one of hydrogen, and so he gave oxygen an atomic weight of 7. In this way, he was able to arrive at the relative weights of the known elements. He wasn't always terribly accurate – oxygen's atomic weight is actually 16, not 7 – but the principle was sound and formed the basis for all of modern chemistry and much of the rest of modern science.

The size of an atom

An individual atom is really impossible to imagine, but let's try:

1. Start with a millimetre, which is a line this long: -
2. Now imagine that line divided into 1,000 equal lengths. (Each of these lengths is a micron.)
3. Divide each micron into 10,000 smaller lengths.
4. You have found the size of an atom: one ten-millionth of a millimetre.

Atoms are tiny – very tiny indeed. Half a million of them lined up shoulder to shoulder could hide behind a human hair.

| Plutonium atomic weight 244 | Iron atomic weight 56 | Hydrogen atomic weight 1 |

A matter of chemistry

Up to the late 1700s, chemistry was almost unknown as a science. It was far more a matter of dabbling with mixtures that would convert the ordinary into the near magical.

In the early days, scientists everywhere were still searching for things that just weren't there, such as the power to bring inanimate objects to life.

The alchemists

Chemists in those days were largely alchemists – scientists who were convinced they could turn common metals into silver or gold. The German Johann Becher went further still. He was certain that, given the right materials, he could make himself invisible. Even stranger, another German, Hennig Brand, collected 50 buckets of human urine which he kept for months in his cellar. By various processes, he converted the urine first into a smelly paste and then into a waxy substance. None of it yielded gold, of course, but a strange and interesting thing did happen. After a time, the substance began to glow. Moreover, when exposed to air, it often spontaneously burst into flame. He hadn't got his gold, but he had discovered phosphorus.

Killer chemistry

In the 1750s, a Swedish chemist named Karl Scheele went on to discover eight elements. Elements in chemistry are substances made up of just one kind of atom and it was Scheele who found chlorine, manganese, nitrogen and oxygen amongst others. He was the first to see that chlorine could be used as a bleach. Sadly, he had an unfortunate habit of tasting the poisons he worked with and succeeded in killing himself this way.

In the early 1800s, there was a fashion in England for inhaling nitrous oxide, or laughing gas, but it would be half a century before anyone got around to using it as an anaesthetic. Goodness knows how many tens of thousands of people suffered agonies under the surgeon's knife because no one had thought of the gas's obvious use.

A head for hydrogen

It was clear that chemistry had a long way to go. Someone clever was needed to thrust it into the modern age. Antoine-Laurent Lavoisier was a French nobleman who worked for a very unpopular institution that collected taxes and fees on behalf of the government. The company didn't tax the rich but only the poor; however, it did provide Lavoisier with the funds to pursue his main interest – science. (At his peak, his personal earnings reached about £12 million in today's money.)

Although Lavoisier didn't discover any elements himself, he did make sense of the discoveries of others. He identified oxygen and hydrogen and gave them both their modern names. One important thing he also established was that a rusting object doesn't lose weight, as everyone had long assumed, but gains it – an extraordinary discovery. Somehow, as it rusted, the object was attracting elemental particles from the air. It was the first realization that matter can be transformed from one kind of thing into another. It can't just be got rid of.

Rival's revenge

Unfortunately, Lavoisier made some dismissive remarks about the theories of a hopeful young scientist named Jean-Paul Marat. The facts were indeed wrong, but Marat never forgave him. In 1793, when Marat had become a leading figure in the French Revolution, he took great pleasure in sending Lavoisier to his death on the dreaded guillotine.

Electrifying liquids

In England, a brilliant young man named Humphry Davy began to bang out new elements, one after another – potassium, sodium, magnesium, calcium, strontium and aluminium. He discovered so many elements not because he was extraordinarily clever, but because he developed an ingenious technique of applying electricity to a liquid substance – electrolysis, as it is known today. Altogether, Davy discovered a dozen elements, a fifth of the known total of his day.

If you burned this book now, its matter would be changed to ash and smoke, but the total amount of 'stuff' in the universe would be the same.

So chemistry was now a serious business, with more chemical elements than it knew what to do with. It would take a new face on the scene to put them in order.

The Periodic Table

Despite the occasional tidyings-up, chemistry was in something of a mess. Because the early chemists worked largely as individuals, they didn't share a common vocabulary. For example, until well into the mid-1800s, the formula H_2O_2 might have meant water to one chemist but hydrogen peroxide to another. There was hardly an element that was represented in the same way everywhere.

Chemists used a bewildering variety of symbols and abbreviations which they just made up as they went along.

Mendeleyev placed his elements into groups of seven. He was said to have been inspired by the card game known as solitaire in North America and patience elsewhere. In the game, cards are arranged by suit, horizontally, and by number, vertically.

Mother Mendeleyev and son

So everybody was very pleased when, in 1869, an odd and crazed-looking professor at the University of St Petersburg in Russia, named Dmitri Ivanovich Mendeleyev, got things sorted out. Mendeleyev was born in the far west of Siberia, the youngest of a very large family. Luck was not always with the Mendeleyevs. When Dmitri was small his father, the headmaster of a local school, went blind and his mother had to go out to work. Clearly an extraordinary woman, she eventually became the manager of a successful glass factory. All went well until 1848, when the factory burned down and the family was reduced to poverty. Determined to get her youngest child an education, the stout-hearted Mrs Mendeleyev hitchhiked 4,000 miles to St Petersburg and deposited young Dmitri at college there.

Laying the table

At the time, elements were normally grouped in two ways: either by their atomic weight – the number of protons plus neutrons in the nucleus of each of their atoms – or by their common properties – whether they were metals or gases, for instance. Mendeleyev's breakthrough was to see that the two could be combined in a single table. Because the properties repeated themselves periodically, the system became known as the **Periodic Table**.

It's elementary!

There was still a great deal that wasn't known or understood. Hydrogen is the most common element in the universe and yet no one would guess as much for another 30 years. Helium, the second most abundant element, wasn't found on Earth until 1895. In fact, another 60 or so elements had yet to be discovered and others may still be waiting to be found.

However, thanks to Mendeleyev's invention, chemistry was now on a firm footing. For chemists, the Periodic Table established an immediate sense of order that can hardly be overstated.

Today we have 117 known elements – 94 naturally occurring ones plus 23 that have been created in labs.

The Periodic Table of Elements

The elements are arranged in horizontal rows called periods, and in vertical columns called groups. This instantly shows one set of relationships when read up and down, and another when read from side to side.
The elements are known by either one or two letters. **As** is the abbreviation for the poisonous element arsenic.

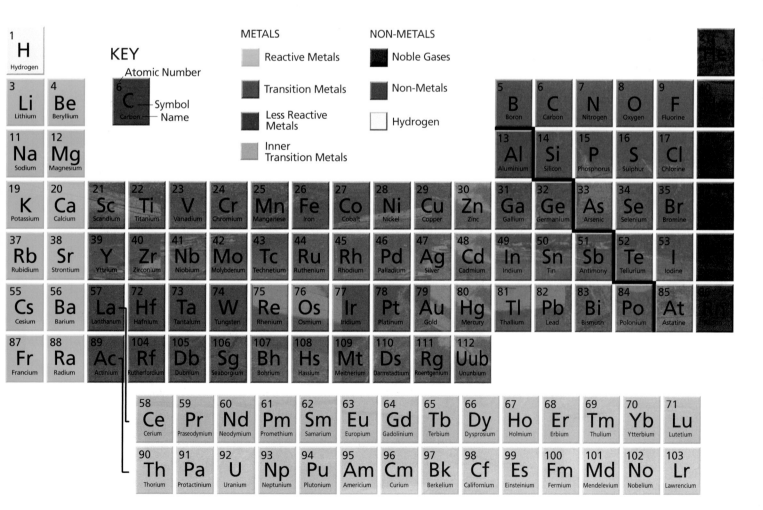

Glowing elements

The 1800s held one last important surprise for chemists. It began in Paris in 1896, when Henri Becquerel left a packet of uranium salts on a wrapped photographic plate in a drawer. When he took the plate out some time later, he was surprised to discover that the salts had burned an impression in it, just as if the plate had been exposed to light. The salts were giving off rays of some sort.

In the process of their work, the Curies found two new elements – polonium, which they named after Marie's native country, Poland, and radium.

Radioactivity is so harmful and long-lasting that even now Marie Curie's papers are too dangerous to handle. Her lab books are kept in lead-lined boxes and those who wish to see them must put on protective clothing.

Warmth from the rocks

Considering the importance of what he had found, Becquerel did a very strange thing: he turned the matter over to a young graduate student named Marie Curie. Working with her husband, Pierre, Marie Curie found that certain kinds of rocks poured out constant and extraordinary amounts of energy, yet they didn't become smaller or change in any noticeable way. What she and her husband couldn't know – what no one would know until Einstein explained things ten years later – was that the rocks were converting mass into energy in an exceedingly efficient way.

Marie Curie dubbed the effect 'radioactivity'.

Killer rays

For a long time it was assumed that anything so miraculously energetic as radioactivity must be beneficial. We now know different! In the early 1900s, Pierre Curie began to experience signs of radiation sickness, and although his wife went on working with distinction in the field, she died of leukaemia brought on by exposure to the rays.

The Sun is a powerful source of radioactive rays. Fortunately, we are protected from these by the layers of gases in our atmosphere.

The luminous paint on the hands and numerals of this 1950s wristwatch contains a small quantity of radium bromide. The paint will continue to glow for many centuries, producing a dangerous gas – one of the reasons why radium in luminous paint is no longer used.

For years, manufacturers of toothpaste and laxatives put a radioactive substance in their products, and at least until the late 1920s one hotel in New York featured with pride the health-giving benefits of its 'radioactive mineral springs'.

Earth keeps itself warm

In Montreal, Canada, a young New Zealander called Ernest Rutherford became interested in the new radioactive materials. He discovered that huge reserves of energy were bound up in these small amounts of matter, and that as the reserves decayed and this energy was released, it accounted for most of where Earth's warmth came from.

Hiding its age

Meanwhile, the guesswork had raged on about the age of Earth, with rock and fossil daters arguing amongst themselves. Nothing in physics could explain how a body the size of the Sun could burn continuously for more than a few tens of millions of years without exhausting its fuel. It followed, therefore, that the Sun and its planets had to be quite young. It was Ernest Rutherford who produced pretty well irrefutable evidence as to why this was wrong.

Radiation 'clock'

Rutherford noticed that in any sample of radioactive material, it always took the same amount of time for half the sample to decay – and that this steady, reliable rate of decay could be used as a kind of clock. By calculating backwards from how much radiation a material had now, and how swiftly it was decaying, you could work out its age. He tested a piece of pitchblende, the principal ore of uranium, and found it to be 700 million years old – very much older than the age most people had been prepared to grant the Earth.

As the 1800s drew to a close, scientists were satisfied that they had pinned down most of the mysteries of the physical world: electricity, magnetism, gases . . . Many wise people believed that there was nothing much left for science to do.

Einstein - the genius

The world was about to enter a century of science where many people wouldn't understand anything and no one would understand everything. One scientist would be responsible for this – Albert Einstein. In 1905, the first of his great scientific papers was published, the famous 'Special Theory of Relativity'. This would solve several of the deepest mysteries of the universe.

$E = mc^2$

Einstein's famous equation did not appear with the paper, but came in a brief supplement that followed a few months later. As you know from listening attentively in class, **E** in the equation stands for energy, **m** for mass and **c²** for the speed of light squared. In simplest terms, what the equation says is that mass and energy are two forms of the same thing. Since **c²** is a truly enormous number, there is a huge amount – a really huge amount – of energy bound up in every material thing.

Explosive power

If you are an average-sized kid you will contain within your modest frame enough potential energy to explode with the force of a large number of very large hydrogen bombs – assuming you want to! Everything has this kind of energy trapped within it.

Mass to energy

Among much else, Einstein's theory explained how radiation worked: how a lump of uranium could throw out constant streams of high-level energy without melting away like an ice cube. It explained how stars could burn for billions of years without racing through their fuel. At a stroke and in a simple formula, Einstein gave geologists and astronomers the luxury of billions of years for the age of the universe.

A brain too brilliant

Almost at once, Einstein's theories developed a reputation for being impossible for an ordinary person to grasp. Even scientists found themselves adrift in a world of particles and anti-particles, where things popped in and out of existence in spans of time that made nanoseconds look plodding. The problem with relativity in particular wasn't that it involved a lot of equations and other complicated mathematics, though it did – even Einstein needed help with some of it – but that it was so intellectually challenging.

The Theory of Relativity

The mathematician and philosopher Bertrand Russell asked people to imagine a train 100 yards long moving at 60 per cent of the speed of light. To someone standing on a platform watching it pass, the train would appear to be only about 80 yards long and everything on it would be squeezed up.

If we could hear the passengers on the train speak, their voices would sound slurred, like a record played too slow, and their movements would appear heavy. Even the clocks on the train would seem to be running at only four-fifths of their normal speed. However – and here's the thing – to the people on the train everything would seem quite normal. It would be us on the platform who looked compressed and slowed down.

Proof that the speed of light is constant actually occurs every time you move. Fly from London to New York and you will step from the plane a quinzillionth of a second younger than the friends you left behind.

Such changes are much too small to make the tiniest detectable difference to us, but for other things in the universe – light, gravity, the universe itself – they are really significant.

Einstein said that space and time are not fixed, but relative both to the observer and to the thing being observed. In fact, as we are about to discover, time even has a shape.

Spacetime

The most challenging of all Einstein's concepts is the idea that time is part of space. Our instinct is to believe that nothing can disturb its steady tick. In fact, according to Einstein, time is variable and ever-changing. It even has shape.

Back to gravity

Spacetime is usually explained by asking you to imagine something flat but soft and bendy – a mattress, say, or a sheet of stretched rubber – on which is resting a heavy round object, such as an iron ball. The weight of the iron ball causes the material on which it is sitting to stretch and sag slightly.

Time warp

This is roughly the effect that a massive object such as the Sun (the iron ball) has on spacetime (the material): it stretches and curves and warps it. Now, if you roll a smaller ball across the sheet, it tries to go in a straight line, but as it nears the iron ball, it rolls downwards, drawn to the more massive object. This is gravity – a product of the bending of spacetime.

A moving cosmos

At about this time, an astronomer with the cheerily intergalactic name of Vesto Slipher (who was in fact not from outer space but from Indiana, USA) was taking spectrograph readings of distant stars and discovering that they appeared to be moving away from us.

The stars Slipher looked at showed unmistakable signs of that distinctive stretched-out 'yee-yummm' sound Formula 1 cars make as they flash past on a racetrack. The phenomenon also applies to light, and in the case of receding galaxies, it is known as a red-shift. Slipher was one of the first to notice this effect with light and to realize its importance for understanding movements in the cosmos. The universe wasn't static, it seemed. Stars and galaxies showed visible colour and were clearly on the move.

Red-shift

Light moving away from us shifts towards the red end of the spectrum. Approaching light shifts to blue.

Yee-yummm!

Johann Christian Doppler, an Austrian physicist, first noticed the effect that bears his name. Briefly, what happens is that as a moving object approaches a stationary one, its sound waves become bunched up. They cram up against whatever device is receiving them – your ears, say. This is heard by you as a kind of high, pinched sound (the *yee*). As the sound source passes, the sound waves spread out and lengthen, causing the pitch to drop (the *yummm*).

The big picture

The American Edwin Hubble was born ten years after Einstein. He would become the most outstanding astronomer of the 1900s, tackling two of the most fundamental questions of the universe: how old is it and precisely how big?

'Candle signposts'

To answer both questions, it is necessary to know two things – how far away certain galaxies are and how fast they are flying away from us. The red-shift gives the speed at which galaxies are moving away, but doesn't tell us how far away they are to begin with. For that you need what are known as 'standard candles' – stars whose brightness can be reliably calculated and used as benchmarks to measure the brightness, and hence relative distance, of other stars.

Henrietta Swan Leavitt studied photographic plates of stars. She found certain stars that were constant points in the sky, and named them 'standard candles'. She used them as a way to measure the larger universe.

Using the work of a brilliant female astronomer, Henrietta Swan Leavitt, as well as Vesto Slipher's handy red-shifts, Hubble began to measure selected points in space. In 1923, he showed that a puff of distant gossamer in the Andromeda constellation, known as M31, wasn't a gas cloud at all, but a blaze of stars. It was a galaxy in its own right – 100,000 light years across and at least 900,000 light years away.

The universe was vaster than anyone had ever supposed.

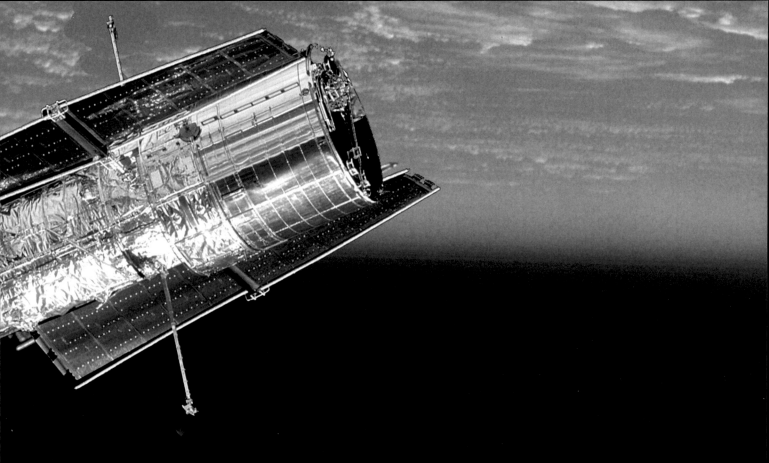

A galaxy of galaxies

In 1919, when Hubble first put his eye to his telescope, the number of galaxies that were known to us was exactly one: the Milky Way. Five years later, he produced a landmark paper showing that the universe consisted not just of the Milky Way but of lots of independent galaxies, many of them bigger than the Milky Way and far more distant. (Astronomers today believe there are perhaps 140 billion galaxies in the visible universe.)

Our expanding universe

This finding alone would have ensured Hubble's reputation, but he now turned to the question of working out just how much vaster the universe was, and made an even more striking discovery. Hubble began to measure the colours on the spectrum of distant galaxies – the business that Slipher had begun. Using a new two-and-a-half-metre diameter telescope, he worked out that all the galaxies in the sky (except for our own local cluster) are moving away from us. Moreover, their speed and distance were neatly proportional: the further away the galaxy, the faster it was moving. Hubble had made a truly startling discovery: that the universe was expanding, swiftly and evenly in all directions.

The Hubble Space Telescope is a large, space-based observatory which has revolutionized astronomy by providing clear views of extremely remote 'baby' galaxies that were forming not long after the Big Bang 13.7 billion years ago.

Far from being the stable, fixed, eternal void that everyone had always assumed, this was a universe that had a beginning. It might therefore also have an end.

'Bad' science

If it had been left to Thomas Midgley, Junior, the end of our planet might have come even faster than it yet may. Midgley was an engineer by training and the world would no doubt have been a safer place if he had stayed so. Instead, he developed an interest in the industrial applications of chemistry and went on to do a great deal of damage to the planet.

Even though lead was widely known to be dangerous, it was still found in many consumer products even into the 1900s. Food came in cans sealed with lead solder. Water was often stored in lead-lined tanks. Lead was sprayed onto fruit as a pesticide. Lead even came as part of toothpaste tubes.

THE GOOD NEWS

Leaded petrol is now banned in most countries and lead levels in people's blood have fallen dramatically. But because lead lasts for ever, modern Americans, for example, each have about 625 times more lead in their blood than people did a century ago. Regrettably, the amount of lead in the atmosphere grows by more than a hundred thousand tonnes a year from industries that continue to use it.

Killing the people

In 1921, while working for the General Motors Research Corporation in Dayton, Ohio, USA, Midgley investigated a mixture of elements called tetraethyl lead and discovered that it reduced the juddering in car engines known as engine knock. What he chose to ignore, however, was that lead, when added to motor fuel, can damage the human brain and central nervous system beyond repair. Among the many symptoms of lead poisoning are blindness, insomnia, kidney failure, hearing loss, cancer and convulsions. In its most acute form it produces terrifying hallucinations, which bring on coma and death.

On the other hand, lead was easy and cheap to extract and hugely profitable to produce industrially – and there was no doubt it did stop engines from knocking. So in 1923, three of America's largest corporations set up the Ethyl Gasoline Corporation with a view to making as much tetraethyl lead as the world was willing to buy, and introducing it into petrol.

Almost at once production workers began to fall ill. As rumours circulated about the dangers, ethyl's inventor, Thomas Midgley, publicly poured it over his hands and sniffed it from a beaker for 60 seconds, to demonstrate how harmless it was. In fact, Midgley knew the perils only too well: he'd been made seriously ill from it a few months earlier and now never went near the stuff if he could help it.

Killing the atmosphere

Buoyed by the success of leaded petrol, Midgley turned to another technological problem of the age. Refrigerators in the 1920s were often appallingly risky because they used dangerous gases that sometimes seeped out. Midgley set out to create a gas that was stable, non-flammable, non-corrosive and safe to breathe. With an instinct for getting it wrong that was almost uncanny, he invented chlorofluorocarbons, or CFCs. Not until half a century later did scientists discover that CFCs were devouring the ozone in the stratosphere. A single kilogram of CFCs can capture and destroy 70,000 kilograms of atmospheric ozone and does about 10,000 times more damage than the same amount of carbon dioxide.

Fragile friend

Ozone is a form of oxygen in which each molecule bears three atoms of oxygen instead of the normal two. Although at ground level it is a pollutant, way up in the stratosphere it is beneficial since it soaks up dangerous ultraviolet radiation from the Sun and prevents Earth from over-heating. But there's not much of it. If all the ozone in the stratosphere were brought down to sea-level, it would form a layer just two millimetres thick.

Satellite sensation

Satellite instruments monitor the ozone layer, which lies between 13 and 21 kilometres above the Earth's surface. This image from NASA, taken in 2006, shows the extent of the ozone hole. It stretches over the whole of the Antarctic region – about 17 million square kilometres. The blue and purple colours show where there is the least ozone, and the greens and yellows are where there is more.

CFCs may ultimately prove to be just about the worst invention of the twentieth century.

THE BAD NEWS

CFCs have been banned in most countries, but they are tenacious little devils and will almost certainly be around and devouring ozone for many tens of years to come. Worse, we are still introducing huge amounts into the atmosphere every year. CFCs are still made overseas and will not be banned in some countries until 2010.

71

A meteoric age

By the 1940s, scientists were at last getting close to dating Earth. One, Willard Libby, was busily inventing radiocarbon dating, a process that would allow scientists to get an accurate reading of the age of bones and other organic remains, something they had never been able to do before.

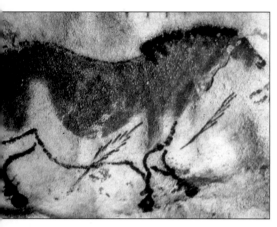

Up until 1940, the oldest reliable dates went back no further than about 3000 BC. No one could confidently say, for instance, when the last ice sheets had retreated, or at what time in the past our early ancestors, who lived up to 45,000 years ago, had decorated the caves of Lascaux in France.

Carbon dating

Libby's idea was based on the realization that all living things contain a special kind of radioactive carbon called carbon-14, which begins to decay at a steady rate as its atoms start to die. Since half of the atoms in carbon-14 decay over a period of 5,600 years, this is known as its half-life. Libby was able to work out how much carbon-14 was left in any dead object and get a good fix on its age. However, he could only do this for objects up to about 40,000 years old.

In fact, there were lots of problems with carbon dating, and with every other technique that followed it. Even the best of these couldn't date anything older than about 200,000 years. But most of all, these techniques couldn't date inorganic materials like rocks, which is, of course, what you need to do if you wish to determine the age of your planet.

Dating ores

Uranium is a very heavy (dense) metal said to have formed in supernovae about 6.6 billion years ago. It is a radioactive element found in many rocks in the Earth's crust.

So it was left to a man called Clair Patterson to come up with the solution. He began work on the project in 1948, making very precise measurements of the lead–uranium ratios in specially selected rocks. These had to be rocks that were extremely ancient and contained lead- and uranium-bearing crystals that were about as old as the planet itself – anything much younger would obviously give misleadingly youthful dates. Patterson's problem was that really ancient rocks are only rarely found on Earth.

Meteorite measures

Eventually, and ingeniously, it occurred to him that he could get round the rock shortage by using rocks from beyond Earth. He turned to meteorites. The assumption he made – rather a large one, but correct as it turned out – was that many meteorites are essentially left-over building materials from the early days of the solar system, and thus still more or less in their original state. Measure the age of these wandering rocks and you would also have the age of the Earth.

It took Patterson seven years of patient work just to find and measure suitable samples for final testing. By this time, he had his specimens, containing minute quantities of uranium and lead locked up in ancient crystals – and he was able to tell the world that the definitive age for the Earth was 4,550 million years (plus or minus 70 million years) – a figure we are still working to today. The Earth finally had an age!

Meteors can be anything from a fraction of a millimetre to the size of a football pitch, and bigger. When a meteor enters Earth's atmosphere, it burns up, flashing across the sky. If it crashes to the ground, it is called a meteorite.

So, here we are . . .

We've come a long way, thanks to some clever geologists, physicists, chemists and astronomers who've helped us work a few things out.

When we started this section we had some hard facts about how big, how round, how heavy and how far from its neighbours in the solar system Earth was. But the one fact that had escaped scientists was how old it was. By working with a lot of old bones, and a great deal of chemistry, they finally got there.

What we know so far:

- that all matter is made up of atoms;
- that substances known as elements make up Earth and its atmosphere;
- that the ancient remains of creatures and plants are preserved as fossils;
- that fossils can help date the rocks that make up the planet;
- that our Earth is very old – 4,550 million years old in fact;
- that galaxies are constantly shifting and moving.

How old is Earth?

1785 James Hutton suggests that Earth's internal upheavals had shaped the planet over a very considerable length of time and that it was far older than anyone had yet dreamed. His ideas paved the way for the birth of geology.

1795 Georges Cuvier assembles fossilized bones into an animal he calls a mastodon.

1796 William Smith works out that fossils embedded in rock layers can be used to date Earth.

1807 The Geological Society is founded in London, UK, where gentlemen meet to dine and discuss the latest scientific craze – geology.

1808 John Dalton confirms that atoms have a size, a shape and that they fit together.

1812 Mary Anning spots and assembles fossils and makes a huge contribution to the science of rock dating.

1830–33 Charles Lyell suggests that Earth had evolved slowly and over a long period of time, and that all geography and geology would support that.

1869 Dmitri Ivanovich Mendeleyev organizes the known elements into a Periodic Table.

1890s Pierre and Marie Curie discover radiation but fail to see how damaging it is to their health.

1905 Albert Einstein produces the Theory of Relativity to explain how we judge time and speed, and suggests $E = mc^2$ to explain how energy is given off.

1912 Vesto Slipher is the first to see that the stars are shifting through the spectrum from blue to red, and is the discoverer of galactic red-shift.

1923 Thomas Midgley does a whole lot of damage to the planet with lead and CFCs.

1930s Edwin Hubble confirms that the universe is full of many moving and expanding galaxies.

1953 Clair Patterson puts the world at 4,550 million years old.

What we don't know:

The upshot of all this is that we live in a universe whose age we can't quite compute, surrounded by stars whose distances from us and each other we don't altogether know, filled with matter we can't identify, operated by physical laws whose properties we don't truly understand.

So let's return to planet Earth and consider something that we do understand – sort of.

Travelling trilobites

By the early 1900s, geologists had decided how old their planet was by examining its rocks and fossils. But they weren't quite finished with Earth yet. A German meteorologist named Alfred Wegener had begun wondering why certain animal fossils repeatedly turned up on opposite sides of oceans that were clearly too wide to swim.

Snails and marsupials

How, he wondered, had marsupials travelled from South America to Australia? How did identical snails turn up in Scandinavia and the east coast of America? Why was one particular species of trilobite that was well-known in Europe also found in Newfoundland – but only on one side? If it had managed to cross 3,000 kilometres of ocean, why couldn't it find its way around the corner of an island just 300 kilometres wide? Just as difficult to explain was another species of trilobite found in Europe and the northwest Pacific coast of America, but nowhere in between.

On the move

Wegener developed the theory that the world's continents had once existed as a single land mass he called Pangaea. Here, plants and animals had been able to mingle before splitting apart and floating off to their present positions.

Unfortunately, he could offer no convincing explanation for how the land masses had moved about, so most scientists stuck to their belief that the continents had occupied their present positions for ever.

At the time, two explanations were popular:

1. The baked-apple theory

This suggested that as the molten Earth cooled, it had become wrinkled like a baked apple, creating ocean basins and mountain ranges. This didn't explain why the wrinkles weren't evenly spaced across the face of the Earth or why, if it had cooled, there was so much heat still left inside it.

2. The land-bridge theory

This suggested that the seas had once been much lower and land bridges had existed between the continents, allowing plants and animals to pass from one to the other. These ancient 'land bridges' were invented and placed wherever needed. When an ancient horse named hipparion was found to have lived in France and Florida at the same time, a land bridge was drawn across the Atlantic. When it was realized that ancient tapirs had existed at the same time in South America and Southeast Asia, a land bridge was drawn there too. Soon, maps of prehistoric seas were almost solid with land bridges – criss-crossing from North America to Europe, from Brazil to Africa.

From here to there

Even now, scientists still worry that species of plants and animals from the ancient worlds have a habit of appearing where they shouldn't and failing to be where they ought. A Triassic reptile called lystrosaurus has been found all the way from Antarctica to Asia, but has never turned up in South America or Australia.

Crust crunching

Africa

South America

Back in 1908, an American geologist named Frank Bursley Taylor was struck by the similarity in shape between the facing coastlines of Africa and South America. Could they once have been joined together?

Crunching mountains

He developed the idea that the continents had once slid around and, as they moved, crunched together. It was these powerful collisions that had thrust up the world's mountain chains. However, since he failed to produce much in the way of evidence, the theory was dismissed as crackpot! Today, in the age of plate tectonics, we can see how close to the mark he actually was.

Drifting continents

Earth's whole crust is in motion, and with it the tectonic plates, as they are known, that form its surface layer. This is made up of eight to twelve big plates, and twenty or so smaller ones. Some are large and comparatively inactive, others small and energetic, but they are all moving in different directions and at different speeds. The constant turmoil of the Earth's crust keeps the plates from fusing into a single immobile plate.

These movements are happening now. As we sit here, continents are truly adrift, like leaves on a pond.

225 million years ago

135 million years ago

Present day

Rocks get around

The connections between modern land masses and those of the past are infinitely more complicated than anyone had imagined. Kazakhstan, in central Asia, was once attached both to Norway and to New England in the USA. One corner of New York, but only a corner, is European. Pick up a pebble from a Massachusetts beach and its nearest kin is in Africa.

The size and shape of the plates often bear little relationship to the land masses that sit upon them. The North American plate, for instance, is much larger than the continent linked to it. Iceland is split down the middle, which makes it half American and half European in tectonic terms. New Zealand, meanwhile, is part of the immense Indian Ocean plate, even though it is nowhere near the Indian Ocean.

All change!

Thanks to Global Positioning Systems, we can see that Europe and North America are parting at about the speed a fingernail grows – roughly two metres in a human lifetime. Eventually, much of California will float off and become an island in the Pacific. Africa has been slowly colliding with Europe for millions of years, pushing up the Alps and Pyrenees mountains. It will squeeze the Mediterranean out of existence, thrust up a chain of mountains of Himalayan size, from Paris to Calcutta, and cause earthquakes in Greece and Turkey. Australia will connect to Asia. The Atlantic Ocean will expand until it is much bigger than the Pacific.

The Earth's crust isn't one complete layer. It is made up of a number of large (and several smaller) shifting tectonic plates, a bit like a cracked eggshell. The whole earth suddenly made sense.

In 150 million years' time

In 250 million years' time

Look at a globe, and what you are really seeing is a snapshot of the continents as they have been for just one-tenth of 1% of the Earth's history.

All adrift

Apart from these strange fossil journeys, there was one other major problem with Earth theories that no one had come close to resolving. That was the question of where all the sediment went. Every year the Earth's rivers carried massive volumes of eroded material – 500 million tonnes of calcium, for instance – to the seas.

Where was it all going?

If you multiplied the rate of this dumping by the number of years it had been going on, there should be about 20 kilometres of sediment on the ocean bottoms – or, put another way, the ocean bottoms should by now be well above the ocean tops.

An Atlantic surprise

People laying ocean-floor cables from Britain to America in the 1800s had already found some kind of mountainous upheaval going on in the mid-Atlantic, and the overall scale of this was a stunning surprise. There was a canyon – a rift – up to 20 kilometres wide running its entire length. The rift went on, tracing a continuous path along the world's sea beds, rather like the pattern on a tennis ball. Occasionally, its higher peaks poked above the water as an island or archipelago – such as the Azores and Canaries in the Atlantic or Hawaii in the Pacific. When all its branches were added together, it extended 75,000 kilometres, lying hidden and unsuspected under thousands of fathoms of salty sea.

Underwater mountains

By the 1950s, oceanographers were undertaking more and more sophisticated surveys of the sea bed. They were discovering that the ocean floor was scored everywhere with canyons, trenches and crevasses and dotted with evidence of volcanoes. They even found a bigger surprise: the mightiest and most extensive mountain range on Earth was – mostly – under water.

Back to the bowels

Then, in 1963, two geophysicists, Drummond Matthews and Fred Vine, finally settled the matter. They proved that the sea floors were splitting and spreading. The Atlantic floor, for example, was acting like two large conveyor belts, one carrying crust towards North America, the other carrying crust towards Europe. New ocean crust was being formed on either side of the central rift, then being pushed away from it as more new crust came along behind. When the crust reached the end of its journey at the boundary with continents, it plunged back into the Earth.

The constant sea-floor spreading explained where all the sediment went. It was being returned to the bowels of the Earth.

The fire below

Plate tectonics explain not only the surface movements of the Earth but also many of its internal actions, such as volcanoes and earthquakes. Even so, we know amazingly little about what happens beneath our feet.

45-minute drop

In fact, we seem to know more about the interior of the Sun than we do about the interior of our own planet. Scientists are generally agreed that the world beneath us is composed of four layers – a rocky outer crust, a mantle of hot, viscous rock, a liquid outer core and a solid inner core. The distance from the surface of Earth to the middle is 6,370 kilometres, which isn't that far. It's been calculated that if you sank a well to the centre and dropped a brick down it, it would take 45 minutes for it to hit the bottom.

Down, down, down!

Our own attempts to penetrate towards the middle of the Earth have been modest. One or two South African gold mines descend to a depth of more than 3,000 metres, but most mines go no further than about 400 metres beneath the surface. If the planet were an apple, we wouldn't yet have broken through the skin. In 1962, Russian scientists drilled to a record 12,000 metres – not even a third of the way through the crust.

The rocky outer crust

The Earth's crust is five to ten kilometres thick under the oceans and thicker – about 40 kilometres – under the land. This is the bit we can examine most easily – and where all the excitement happens!

The churning mantle

The mantle is 82% of Earth's volume – most of it, in fact. It reaches as far as 3,000 kilometres below us. Rock in the mantle rises and falls in a churning process called convection.

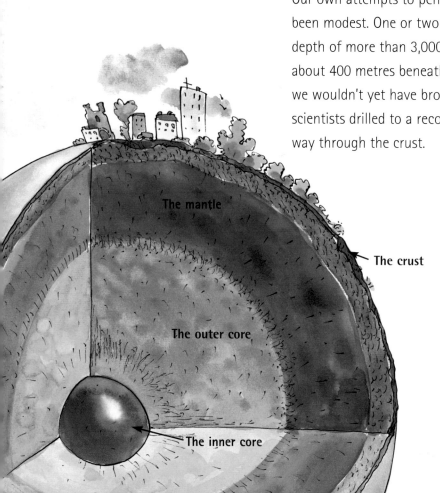

The mantle

The crust

The outer core

The inner core

The liquid outer core

We don't know very much about the outer core, although everyone agrees it is fluid and that it is the seat of magnetism. It revolves in a way that makes it, in effect, an electrical motor, creating Earth's magnetic field.

The solid inner core

Scientists know that the pressures at the centre of the Earth are high enough to turn any rock there solid. They also know that the inner core is very good at holding its heat. It's thought that in over four billion years, the temperature at the core has fallen by no more than 110 °C.

No one knows exactly how hot the Earth's core is. Estimates range from something over 4,000°C to over 7,000°C – about as hot as the surface of the Sun.

Molten rock erupts from the Earth's mantle in the form of red-hot magma.

Boom!

Before . . .

Nothing better demonstrates how little we know about the Earth's interior than how badly we are caught out when it plays up. The eruption of Mount St Helens in Washington State, USA, in 1980 is a good example.

First rumblings

St Helens started its ominous rumblings on 20 March. Within a week it was erupting magma, albeit in modest amounts, up to a hundred times a day, and being constantly shaken by earthquakes. People were evacuated to what was assumed to be a safe distance of 13 kilometres. As the mountain's rumblings grew, St Helens became a tourist attraction. Newspapers gave daily reports on the best places to get a view. Television crews repeatedly flew in helicopters to the summit and people were even seen climbing over the mountain. But as the days passed and the rumblings failed to develop into anything dramatic, people grew restless and decided that the volcano wasn't going to blow after all.

Then, on 19 April, the northern flank of the mountain began to bulge. Remarkably, the seismologists in charge decided it would behave like Hawaiian volcanoes, which don't blow out sideways. Only one person, a geology professor named Jack Hyde, pointed out that St Helens didn't have an open vent at the top, as Hawaiian volcanoes do, so any pressure building up inside was bound to be released dramatically in some other way. But no one paid any attention to him.

After . . .

And then . . .

At 8.32 a.m. on Sunday 18 May, an earthquake caused the north side of the volcano to collapse, sending an enormous avalanche of dirt and rock rushing down the mountain slope at nearly 250 kilometres an hour. It was the biggest landslide in human history and carried enough material to bury the whole of Manhattan to a depth of 120 metres. A minute later, St Helens exploded, releasing the equivalent of 27,000 Hiroshima-sized atomic bombs and shooting out a mysterious hot cloud at over 1,000 kilometres an hour – much too fast for anyone nearby to out-race it.

What happened next . . .

Many people who were thought to be in safe areas, often far out of sight of the volcano, were overtaken. 57 people were killed; 23 of the bodies were never found. The death toll would have been much higher had it not been a Sunday. On any weekday, many lumber workers would have been working within the death zone. 600 square kilometres of forest were devastated. Trees were just blown away! Ash rained down on the nearest town, turning day into night, clogging motors and generators, choking pedestrians and generally bringing things to a halt.

The Yellowstone National Park covers about 9,000 square kilometres. Most of the park is covered in forests; the rest is meadow, lakes and grassland.

There are 10,000 hot springs and geysers in the park – more than in the whole of the rest of the world put together.

Yellowstone Park

There are some people out there who spend their lives hunting for volcanoes. Bob Christiansen of the United States Geological Survey is one of them.

Hunt the caldera

In the 1960s, Bob Christiansen was puzzled about something: he couldn't find the volcano in Yellowstone Park. It had been known for a long time that the park was volcanic – that's what accounted for all its geysers and other steamy features – and the one thing about volcanoes is that they are generally pretty easy to spot. But Christiansen couldn't find the Yellowstone volcano anywhere. In particular, he couldn't find a structure known as a caldera.

Altogether there are some 10,000 visible volcanoes on Earth. More often than not, we see them as cone-shaped hills with lava-strewn slopes. Most of them are extinct, which means they don't erupt any more. But some volcanoes don't erupt and build cones. They explode! These kinds of volcanoes explode in a single mighty rupture, leaving behind a vast, caved-in kind of pit – a caldera. Yellowstone was one of these.
But Christiansen still couldn't find the caldera in Yellowstone Park . . .

NASA to the rescue

Now it just so happened that, at this time, NASA was testing its high-altitude cameras by taking photos of Yellowstone. Copies of these were passed to the park authorities so they could make a nice display for the visitors. As soon as Christiansen saw the photos, he realized why he had failed to spot the caldera – virtually the whole park WAS a caldera! The explosion had left a crater over 60 kilometres across – much too large to be seen from anywhere at ground level.

The hot facts!

- Yellowstone sits on an enormous reservoir of molten rock that begins at least 200 kilometres down and rises to near the surface.
- The heat from the hot spot is what powers all of Yellowstone's vents, geysers, hot springs and mud pots.
- Beneath the surface is a magma chamber that's about 72 kilometres across – roughly the size of the park – full of unstable magma that could blow at any time.
- Since it first erupted 16.5 million years ago, it's blown up about a hundred times. The eruption of two million years ago put out enough ash to bury the whole of California six metres deep.
- Scientists have worked out that Yellowstone blows roughly every 600,000 years. The last time was 630,000 years ago.

Could Yellowstone explode again at any time?
And without warning? Yes, it happens all the time.

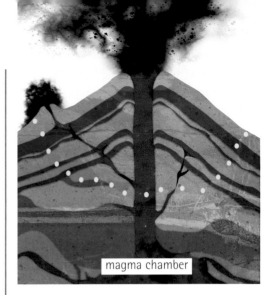

magma chamber

A caldera can form after a volcano has exploded. Once the magma chamber empties, the mountain may collapse in on itself, leaving a large hollow (marked by the yellow dots).

The warning signs

Yellowstone Park already has lots of earthquakes: 1,000 to 3,000 occur every year – not large ones but a definite warning.

The most famous geyser in the park, Excelsior, used to spurt steam 100 metres into the air. In 1890 it just stopped. Then it started again in 1985 for two days and hasn't been active since. These are all signs that the whole park is unpredictable.

Yellowstone Park is a reminder that we live on a very hot and destructive planet!

Big quakes

Earthquakes are unpredictable too and we know very little about what causes them. However, it does appear that as plates collide and other disturbances happen, shock waves penetrate deep into the Earth, then bounce off the core and cause great tremors through the crust.

The Richter scale

It was two American geologists who in 1935 came up with a way to make comparisons between one earthquake and the next. They were Beno Gutenberg and Charles Richter – after whom the scale came to be known.

The Richter scale works in such a way that a 7.3 quake is ten times more powerful than a 6.3 one, and 100 times more powerful than a 5.3 earthquake. The scale is a simple measure of force, but says nothing about damage. A size 7 quake – happening deep in the mantle, say 650 kilometres down – might cause no surface damage at all, while a far smaller one – happening just six or seven kilometres under the surface – could create widespread devastation. Much also depends on how long it lasts, the frequency and strength of aftershocks, and the land it affects.

Three whoppers

There have been lots of big earthquakes since the invention of the Richter scale – for example, one in Alaska in March 1964, which measured 9.2 on the scale, and one in the Pacific Ocean off the coast of Chile in 1960, a truly grand 9.5.

But for pure devastation, the most intense earthquake on record was one that shook the city of Lisbon, Portugal, to pieces in 1755. Just before ten in the morning, it was hit by a sudden sideways lurch, now estimated at magnitude 9.0, and shaken ferociously for six full minutes. Survivors enjoyed just three minutes of calm before a second shock came. A third and final shock followed where the force of the convulsions was so great that the water rushed out of the city's harbour and returned in a wave over 15 metres high, adding to the destruction. At the end of it all, at least 60,000 people were dead and almost all the buildings reduced to rubble.

Tokyo tomorrow?

Tokyo stands on the meeting point of three tectonic plates in Japan, a country already well known for its seismic instability. In 1995, the city of Kobe was struck by a 7.2 quake. The damage was estimated at US$200 billion. But that was nothing compared with what may await Tokyo.

Tokyo has already suffered one of the most devastating earthquakes in modern times. On 1 September 1923, just before midday, the city was hit by what is known as the Great Kanto quake – an event over ten times as powerful as Kobe's earthquake. About 140,000 people were killed. Since that time, Tokyo has been eerily quiet, so the strain beneath the surface has been building for 85 years. Eventually it is bound to snap.

Earthquakes are fairly common. Every day on average, somewhere in the world, there are over 1,000 of magnitude 2.0 or greater – that's enough to give anyone nearby a pretty good jolt.

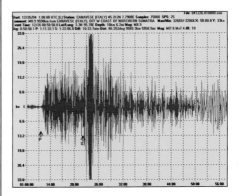

This Richter scale reading shows the quake that sent the seas rushing forward at amazing speed in the 2004 tsunami disaster in Southeast Asia.

Impact from space

For a long time people had known that there was something odd about the earth beneath the town of Manson, Iowa, in the USA. Then, in 1912, a man drilling a well for the town's water supply reported bringing up a lot of strangely shaped rocks. The water was odd, too. It was almost as soft as rainwater, and such natural soft water had never been found in Iowa before.

Asteroid spotter

It took until the early 1950s for the reason to unfold. At this point, a bright young geologist named Eugene Shoemaker paid a visit to a possible meteor crater located in the entirely different state of Arizona, where he found huge distributions of unusual kinds of sandy-grained quartz. This suggested the site had received an impact from space and set off an interest that led him to begin a detailed survey of asteroids that came close to Earth's orbit.

Dinosaur hit

Meanwhile, two geologists, Walter Alvarez and his father, Luis, announced they believed the extinction of the dinosaurs hadn't taken place over millions of years as part of some slow and gradual process, but suddenly, in a single explosive event. They'd made an amazing discovery between two ancient layers of limestone in a hilly area of Umbria in Italy. Here, they'd found evidence of mineral deposits only found in outer space which had, at some point, been deposited on Earth. They could only have arrived there if some huge piece of rock, such as an asteroid, had shattered there, scattering its contents over the site.

The KT boundary

The Alvarez layer of rock is now known as the KT boundary. It marks the time, 65 million years ago, when the dinosaurs, and roughly half the world's other species of animals, abruptly vanished from the fossil record. However, the Alvarezes didn't have an impact site to prove their theory; the Chicxulub crater in Mexico is now thought to be a likely candidate.

The Manson meteor

Some time in the very ancient past, when Manson stood on the edge of a shallow sea, a rock about two and a half kilometres across, weighing 10 billion tonnes and travelling at perhaps 200 times the speed of sound, had ripped through the atmosphere and punched into the Earth with a violence and suddenness that we can scarcely imagine. Where Manson now stands became, in an instant, a hole five kilometres deep and more than 30 kilometres across. And all this had come, not from within the Earth, but from at least 160 million kilometres beyond.

Preserved

The Manson impact was the biggest thing that has ever occurred on the mainland United States. Of any type. Ever. The crater it left behind was so colossal that if you stood on one edge you would only just be able to see the other side on a good day. It would make the Grand Canyon look quaint. Unfortunately, 2.5 million years of passing ice sheets have filled the Manson crater to the top with rich glacial sediment, so that today, the landscape at Manson, and for miles around, is as flat as a tabletop.

Impact on Jupiter

In July 1994, humans were able to witness for the first time the collision between a comet and the planet Jupiter, thanks to the Hubble Space Telescope. The impacts went on for a week and were bigger than expected.

One fragment, known as Nucleus G, struck Jupiter with a force 75 times greater than the explosive power of all the nuclear weapons that exist in the world.

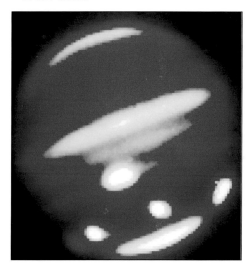

Nucleus G was a rock only about the size of a small mountain, but it created these huge yellow wounds in the surface of Jupiter, each of which is the size of Earth.

Scientists tell us that an impact like Manson happens about once every million years. But don't relax. Earth is still a very precarious place, as we shall find out.

91

Asteroid hit

Asteroids are rocky objects orbiting in loose formation in a belt between Mars and Jupiter. In illustrations, they are always shown as existing in a jumble, but in fact the solar system is quite a roomy place and the average asteroid will actually be over 1,500,000,000 kilometres from its nearest neighbour.

A total disaster!

If a meteor similar to the one at Manson hit us today, it would slam into the Earth's surface one second after entering the atmosphere and would vaporize instantly.

However, the blast would blow out 1,000 cubic kilometres of rock, earth and superheated gases.

Every living thing within 250 kilometres would be killed by the heat or the blast.

The impact would almost certainly set off a chain of devastating earthquakes.

Volcanoes across the globe would begin to rumble and spew.

Tsunamis would rise up and head devastatingly for distant shores.

Within an hour, a cloud of blackness would cover the Earth and burning rock and other debris would be pelting down everywhere, setting much of the planet ablaze.

Nobody knows even approximately how many asteroids there are tumbling through space, but the number is thought to be probably not less than a billion. They are presumed to be planets that never quite made it, owing to the unsettling gravitational pull of Jupiter, which keeps them from joining up.

En route . . . to us

Think of the Earth's orbit as a kind of motorway on which we are the only vehicle, but which is crossed regularly by pedestrians who don't look before stepping off the pavement. At least 90 per cent of these pedestrians are quite unknown to us. We don't know where they live, what sort of hours they keep, how often they come our way. All we know is that, at some point, they trundle across the road down which we are cruising at over 1,000,000 kilometres an hour. Suppose there was a button you could push and you could light up all the asteroids crossing Earth that were larger than about ten metres. Well, there would be over a hundred million of these objects in the sky.

In short, you would see not a couple of thousand distant twinkling stars, but millions upon millions upon millions of closer, moving objects – all of which are capable of colliding with the Earth, and all of which are moving on slightly different courses through the sky and at different rates. It would be deeply unnerving. Well, be unnerved, because they are there. We just can't see them.

A busy highway

Altogether it's thought that some 2,000 asteroids big enough to put us in peril regularly cross our orbit. But even a small asteroid – the size of a house, say – could destroy a city. The number of these relative tiddlers in Earth-crossing orbits is almost certainly in the region of hundreds of thousands, and possibly in the millions – and they are nearly impossible to track.

Duck now!

Let's suppose we did see an object coming. What would we do? Everyone assumes we would send up a nuclear warhead and blast it to smithereens – but there are some problems with that idea. First, our missiles aren't designed for space work. They haven't the oomph to escape Earth's gravity; and even if they did, there are no mechanisms to guide them across tens of millions of kilometres of space. Indeed, we no longer possess a rocket powerful enough to send humans even as far as the Moon. The last rocket that could, *Saturn 5*, was retired years ago.

Even a year's warning would probably be insufficient to take appropriate action. The greater likelihood, however, is that we wouldn't see any object until it was about six months away, which would be much too late.

Near miss

The first asteroid to be spotted was Ceres, in 1801. It was nearly 1,000 km across. In 1991 an asteroid named 1991BA sailed past us at a distance of 160,000 km – in cosmic terms, the equivalent of a bullet passing through one's sleeve without touching the arm.

Two years later, another somewhat larger asteroid missed us by just 150,000 kilometres. The closest yet recorded was the 1994 XLI, which passed by 100,000 km away.

Such near misses probably happen two or three times a week and go unnoticed.

The asteroid Apophis, a 400-metre-wide space rock, will come closer to Earth in 2029 than the orbits of many communications satellites – but it won't hit us.

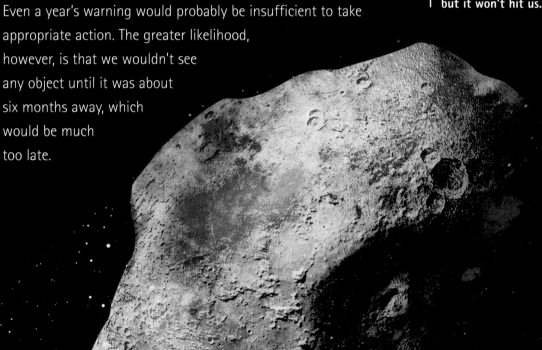

Our tiny patch

For all the uncertainty of the small piece of planet we live on, we should be grateful that we have this patch at all. In the whole universe, as far as we yet know, there is only one place that will sustain us – and that's Earth. But even this can be pretty grudging. Of the small portion of the planet's surface that is dry enough to stand on, a surprisingly large amount is too hot or cold or dry or steep or high up to be of much use to us. Partly, this is our fault.

Helpless humans

Humans are pretty useless at adapting. Like most animals, we don't much like really hot places, but because we sweat so freely and easily succumb to heat strokes, we are especially vulnerable. In the worst circumstances – on foot without water in a hot desert – most people will grow delirious and keel over in less than seven or eight hours. We are equally helpless in the cold. Like all mammals, humans are good at generating heat. However, because we're so nearly hairless, we aren't good at keeping it. Even in quite mild weather, half the calories you burn go to keeping you warm.

Our lucky breaks

Yet when you consider what goes on elsewhere in the known universe, the wonder is that we've managed to find a planet with even a tiny bit to live on. You have only to look at roasting Venus or freezing Mars to appreciate that most places are much harsher than our mild, blue, watery globe. So far, space scientists have only discovered about 250 planets outside our solar system of the possible ten billion trillion or so that exist – but it appears that to have a planet suitable for life, you have to be awfully lucky.

Excellent location

We are, to an almost uncanny degree, the right distance from the right sort of star – one that is big enough to radiate lots of energy, but not so big as to burn itself out swiftly. The larger a star is, the more rapidly it burns. Had our Sun been ten times bigger, it would have exhausted itself after ten million years instead of ten billion, and we wouldn't be here now. We are also fortunate to orbit where we do: 5 per cent nearer or 15 per cent further away from the Sun, and everything on Earth would have boiled away or frozen.

We're a twin planet

Not many of us think of the Moon as a companion planet, but that's what it is. Without it we would wobble like a dying top. The Moon's steady gravitational pull keeps the Earth spinning at the right speed and angle, and stable enough for life to develop. This won't go on for ever. The Moon is slipping from our grasp at a rate of about four centimetres a year. In another two billion years it will have moved so far away that it won't help us at all.

The right kind of planet

But just being the right distance from the Sun isn't the whole story, for otherwise the Moon would be forested and fair, which it clearly isn't. Unlike the Moon, our planet has a molten interior. It's pretty certain that without all that magma swirling around beneath us we wouldn't be here now. Our lively interior created the outpourings of gas that helped to build an atmosphere and provided us with the magnetic field that shields us from cosmic radiation. It also gave us plate tectonics, which continually renew and rumple the surface. If the Earth were perfectly smooth, it would be covered with water to a depth of over three kilometres.

Timing

The universe is an amazingly fickle and eventful place and our existence within it is a wonder. If its long and complex history stretching back 4.6 billion years or so hadn't played out in a particular manner and at particular times – if, for instance, the dinosaurs hadn't been wiped out by a meteorite when they were – you might well be a few centimetres long, with whiskers and a tail, and reading this in a burrow. It seems clear that if you wish to end up as a moderately advanced, thinking society, you need to have enjoyed periods of stability coupled with periods of stress and challenge (the ice ages, for example) and, of course, without encountering a disaster that would wipe you out.

Hot and cold

Temperature is just a measure of how active the molecules in the atmosphere are. At sea level, air molecules are so thick that one molecule can move only the tiniest distance – about eight-millionths of a centimetre – before banging into another. Because trillions of molecules are constantly colliding, a lot of heat is exchanged. But at the height of the thermosphere, the air is so thin that any two molecules will be miles apart and hardly ever come into contact. So although each molecule is very warm, they rarely touch and exchange heat.

Troposphere

The troposphere contains enough warmth and oxygen to allow us to function, but is only about 10–16 kilometres thick. 80% of the atmosphere's mass, virtually all the water, and most of the weather, are within this thin and wispy layer.

Stratosphere

When you see the top of a storm cloud flattening out into an anvil shape, it is at the boundary between the troposphere and the stratosphere. A fast lift would get you there in 20 minutes. However, the pressure change would mean that when the doors opened anyone inside would be dead. The temperature here can be -57°C.

Earth's blanket

Thank goodness for the atmosphere. Without it, Earth would be a lifeless ball of ice with an average temperature of minus 50 degrees Celsius. In addition, the atmosphere absorbs or deflects incoming swarms of cosmic rays, charged particles, ultra-violet rays and the like.

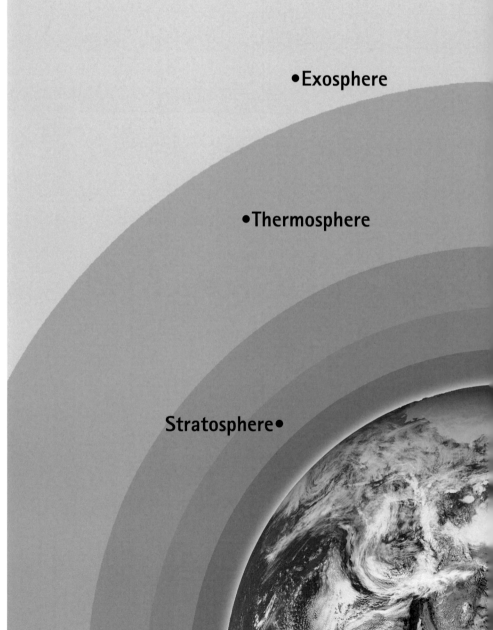

•Exosphere

•Thermosphere

Stratosphere•

A thin armour

The most striking thing about our atmosphere is that there isn't very much of it. It extends upwards for about 190 kilometres, which might seem reasonably generous when viewed from ground level, but if you shrank the Earth to the size of a standard desktop globe, it would only be about the thickness of a couple of coats of varnish.

However, what there is, is tough. Altogether, the gaseous padding of the atmosphere is equivalent to a 4.5-metre thickness of protective concrete. Without it, the invisible cosmic rays from space would slice through us like tiny daggers. Even raindrops would pound us senseless if it weren't for the atmosphere's slowing drag.

•Mesosphere

•Troposphere

Mesosphere

The mesosphere rises just over 80 kilometres above the stratosphere. Here the temperature is even colder, falling as low as 90 degrees below freezing.

Thermosphere

Here, the temperature skyrockets to a boiling 1,500°C as you begin to feel the impact of the Sun with no protective layers between you and it.

Exosphere

From about 500 kilometres up to 10,000 kilometres above the earth, atoms and molecules can escape into space, and charged particles are ejected from the upper atmosphere of the Sun in strong solar winds.

Hugging the ground

But you needn't venture to the edge of the atmosphere to be reminded of what hopelessly Earth-bound beings we are. Many people become severely ill at no more than 4,500 metres or so. We cannot live permanently above 5,500 metres. Even experienced mountaineers, with the benefits of fitness, training and bottled oxygen, quickly become vulnerable, and above 7,500 metres is the area known to climbers as the Death Zone.

In a hundred ways the human body reminds its owner that it isn't designed to operate very far above sea level.

Wild and windy

Air in motion, as with a hurricane or even a stiff breeze, will quickly remind you that it has very considerable mass or weight. Altogether, there are about 5,200 million million tonnes of air around us – 25 million tonnes for every square mile of the planet – that's a lot! When you get millions of tonnes of atmosphere rushing past at 50 or 60 kilometres an hour, it's hardly surprising that tree-limbs snap and roof tiles go flying.

Rising and falling

The process that moves air around in the atmosphere and causes winds, as well as most other weather, is called convection. Moist, warm air from the regions close to the Equator rises until it hits the troposphere, then it spreads out. As it does this, it cools and sinks. Some of the sinking air looks for an area of low pressure to fill and heads back for the Equator, completing the circuit.

Because of this movement, differences in air pressure arise on the planet. Air can't abide this, so it rushes around trying to equalize things everywhere. In fact, weather is the result of an endless battle. Air always flows from areas of high pressure to areas of low pressure, and the greater the variation in pressures, the faster the wind blows.

A tropical hurricane can release in 24 hours as much energy as a rich, medium-sized nation like France uses in a year.

Thunder and lightning

At any one moment, 1,800 thunder-storms are in progress around the globe – some 40,000 a day. Day and night across the planet, about 100 lightning bolts hit the ground each second.

A bolt of lightning travels at 435,000 kilometres an hour and can heat the air around it to a decidedly crisp 28,000 degrees Celsius – several times hotter than the surface of the Sun.

Life cycle of a raindrop

Depending on where it falls, the fate of a water molecule varies widely. If it lands in fertile soil, it will be soaked up by plants or re-evaporated directly within hours or days. If it finds its way down to the groundwater, however, it may not see sunlight again for many years – thousands if it gets really deep. When you look at a lake, you are looking at a collection of molecules that have been there, on average, for about ten years. In the ocean, the residence time is thought to be more like a hundred years.

Altogether, about 60 per cent of water molecules in a rainfall are returned to the atmosphere within a day or two. They spend just over a week in the sky on average, then fall as rain again.

The stuff of clouds

When high- and low-pressure systems meet, you can often tell what's going to happen from the clouds. The father of modern meteorology who in 1803 gave us names for clouds was an English pharmacist named Luke Howard.

In the right conditions, heavy nimbus (rain) clouds can rise to heights of 10 to 15 km and contain updraughts and down-draughts of over 140 km an hour.

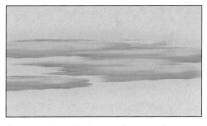

Stratus clouds form when moisture-bearing updraughts lack the oomph to break through a level of more stable air above, and instead spread out, like smoke hitting a ceiling.

A fluffy summer cumulus, several hundred metres across, may contain no more than 100–150 litres of water – enough to fill a bathtub. So only about 0.035% of the Earth's fresh water is floating around above us at any moment.

Cirrus clouds are thin, wisp-like strands that indicate strong winds high in the sky. They are mainly made up of ice crystals and generally presage colder weather.

Hot-water bottle

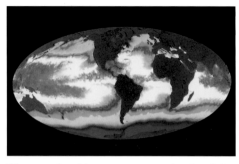

Warm and colder ocean currents circulate around the globe and affect the climate of continents they touch.

The real driving force that dictates what weather will happen on the planet's surface is the oceans. Indeed, meteorologists increasingly treat oceans and atmosphere as a single system, which is why we must give them a little of our attention here.

Water is marvellous at holding and transporting heat – unimaginably vast quantities of it. Every day, the Gulf Stream carries an amount of heat to Europe equivalent to burning the world's output of coal for ten years, which is why Britain and Ireland have such mild winters compared with Canada and Russia. But water also warms slowly, which is why lakes and swimming pools are cold, even on the hottest days.

Sinking salt water

The oceans are not one huge mass of water. There are differences in temperature, salt content, depth, density, and so on. All of these affect how each ocean moves heat around, which in turn affects climate.

The Atlantic, for instance, is saltier than the Pacific. The saltier the water, the denser it is, and dense water sinks. Without its extra burden of salt, the Atlantic currents would proceed up to the Arctic, keeping the North Pole warm, but not Europe. As it happens, the surface waters grow dense and sink as they approach Europe, and then begin a slow trip back to the southern hemisphere. When they reach Antarctica, they are caught up in the continent's main current and driven onward into the Pacific. The process is very slow – it can take 1,500 years for water to travel from the North Atlantic to the mid-Pacific – but the volumes of heat and water that are moved are considerable and the influence on the climate is enormous.

Carbon sponge

The seas do one other great favour for us. They help soak up huge volumes of unhealthy carbon dioxide gas and provide a means for it to be safely locked away. One of the oddities of our solar system is that the Sun burns about a quarter more brightly now than when the solar system was young. So Earth should be a lot warmer. In fact, it should have had a catastrophic effect on things here.

So what keeps the planet stable and cool? Life does. Trillions upon trillions of tiny sea organisms that most of us have never heard of – things called foraminiferans and coccoliths and calcareous algae. These tiny organisms capture the carbon dioxide in the atmosphere when it falls as rain and use it to make their tiny shells. By locking the carbon up in their shells, they keep it from evaporating back into the atmosphere, where it would build up dangerously as a greenhouse gas.

Cliffs of carbon

Eventually, all the tiny foraminiferans and coccoliths and so on die and fall to the bottom of the sea, where they are pressed into limestone. It's remarkable, when you look at an extraordinary natural feature like the White Cliffs of Dover in England, to reflect that they're made up almost entirely of tiny dead marine organisms. What's more incredible is how much carbon they are storing there. A 15-centimetre cube of Dover chalk will contain well over 1,000 litres of compressed carbon dioxide that would otherwise be doing us no good at all.

The White Cliffs of Dover.

Altogether, there's about 80,000 times as much carbon locked away in the Earth's rocks as in the atmosphere.

Awash with water

Imagine trying to live in a world dominated by a liquid that has no taste or smell and that can be both life-giving AND a lethal killer. It can scald you or freeze you. One moment it's in the sky and the next, soaking you to the skin. It can stir itself up into such a fury that it can knock over buildings.
We call it water.

A potato is 80% water, a cow 74%, a bacterium 75%. A tomato, at 95%, is not a lot else but water. Even humans are 65% water, making us more water than solid.

One water cycle

There are 1.3 billion cubic kilometres of water on Earth and that's all we're ever going to get. The water you drink has been around doing its job since the Earth was young. By 3.8 billion years ago, the oceans had more or less filled up and since then it's all been about recycling.

Floating ice

Because it's so familiar, we tend to overlook what an extraordinary substance water is. Most liquids contract by about 10 per cent when chilled. Water does too, but once it's within whispering distance of freezing, it begins, for some reason, to expand. By the time it's solid, it's almost a tenth bulkier than it was before.

Because it expands, it can float on water – which is bizarre because, by rights, it should sink. Of course, if it did, lakes and oceans would freeze from the bottom up. Without surface ice to hold heat in, the water's warmth would radiate away, the oceans would freeze and almost certainly stay that way, probably for ever. Thankfully for us, water seems unaware of the rules of chemistry or the laws of physics.

Sticking together

Everyone knows that water's chemical formula is H_2O, which means that it consists of one largish oxygen atom with two smaller hydrogen atoms attached to it. The hydrogen atoms cling fiercely to their oxygen host, but also link up with other water molecules. That's why water molecules stick together to form puddles and lakes, but don't stick so tightly that they can't be separated when you dive into a pool of them.

Killer salt

Deprived of water, the human body rapidly falls apart. Within days, the lips vanish, the gums blacken, the nose withers to half its length, and the skin contracts around the eyes and prevents blinking. Water is so vital to us that it's easy to forget that most of the water found on Earth is poisonous to us – deadly poisonous – because of the salts in it.

We need salt to live, but only in very small amounts, and sea water contains about 70 times more salt than we can safely take in. A typical litre of sea water will contain only about 2.5 teaspoons of common salt – the kind we sprinkle on food – but much larger amounts of other elements, compounds and other dissolved solids, which are collectively known as salts.

Take a lot of salt into your body and from every cell water molecules rush around like volunteer firemen trying to dilute it and carry it away. This leaves the cells dangerously short of the water they need and they become dehydrated. Meanwhile, the overworked blood cells carry the salt to the kidneys, which eventually become overwhelmed and shut down. Without working kidneys you die. That's why you don't drink sea water.

Sticky water

Because water molecules 'stick together', they can flow uphill when siphoned, or form beads on a car bonnet. This is also why water has surface tension, creating a sort of 'skin' on the surface that is strong enough to support insects like the water strider.

Watery facts

- 97% of all the water on Earth is in the seas, the greater part of it in the Pacific, which is bigger than all the land masses put together.

- Altogether, the Pacific holds just over half of all the ocean water; the Atlantic has about a quarter and the Indian Ocean a little less, leaving just 3.6% to be accounted for by all the other seas.

- The average depth of the ocean is 3.86 kilometres, with the Pacific on average about 300 metres deeper than the Atlantic and Indian oceans.

- Of the 3% of Earth's water that is fresh, only the tiniest amount – 0.036% – is found in lakes, rivers and reservoirs, and an even smaller part – just 0.001% – exists in clouds or as vapour.

- Much of the planet's ice is in Antarctica. Go to the South Pole and you will be standing on over 3,000 metres of ice, at the North Pole just five metres of it.

'Water' would be a more accurate name for our planet than 'Earth'.

103

Down in the deep

We happen to belong to the group of living things that took the rash but adventurous decision 400 million years ago to crawl out of the seas and become land-based oxygen-breathers. As a consequence, 99.5 per cent of the world's habitable space by volume is off limits to us.

Without assistance, the deepest anyone has gone and lived to talk about it afterwards is 86 metres – a good bit shorter than a football pitch. This feat was performed by a New Zealander named William Trubridge, who in April 2008 set the 'constant weight without fins' record in a dive time of 3.2 minutes.

Water pressure

It isn't simply that we can't breathe in water, but that we couldn't bear the pressures. Because water is about 1,300 times heavier than air, pressures rise swiftly as you descend. Nearly everyone assumes that the human body would crumple under the immense pressures of the deep ocean. In fact, because we are made largely of water, the body remains at the same pressure as the surrounding water, and is not crushed at depth. It is the gases inside your body that cause the trouble. If you descended 150 metres underwater, your veins would collapse and your lungs would compress to the size of a drinks can.

Amazingly, people do voluntarily dive to such depths without breathing apparatus, just for the fun of it, in a sport known as free diving. However, they don't stay down long enough for the nitrogen in their system to dissolve into their tissues.

Diving disasters

Plenty else can go wrong. In the days of diving suits – the sort that were connected to the surface by long hoses – divers sometimes experienced a dreaded phenomenon known as 'the squeeze'. This occurred when the surface pumps failed, leading to a catastrophic loss of pressure in the suit. The air would leave the suit with such violence that the unfortunate diver would be sucked up into the helmet and hosepipe. When hauled to the surface, all that was left in the suit was bones and some rags of flesh!

The real terror of the deep, however, is 'the bends'.

Body bubbles

The air we breathe contains 80 per cent nitrogen. Put the human body under pressure, and that nitrogen is transformed into tiny bubbles that migrate into the blood and tissues. If the pressure is changed too rapidly – as with a too-quick ascent by a diver – the bubbles trapped within the body will begin to fizz in exactly the manner of a freshly opened bottle of lemonade. They clog tiny blood vessels, depriving cells of oxygen, and cause pain so excruciating that sufferers are prone to bend double in agony – hence 'the bends'.

Sturdy shrimp

Other creatures manage to deal with the pressures at depth, although how some of them do so is a mystery. The deepest point in the ocean is the Mariana Trench in the Pacific. There, some 11 kilometres down, the pressures rise to 1,125 kilograms per square centimetre. We have managed just once, briefly, to send humans to that depth in a sturdy diving vessel, yet it's home to a crustacean, similar to a shrimp, which survives without any protection at all.

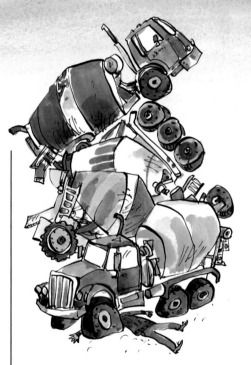

Even at the average ocean depth of four kilometres, the pressure is the same as being squashed beneath 14 loaded cement trucks.

Protein soup

As we have seen, oceans are uninviting places. However, it was in the oceans that life got going in the first place. And it's safe to say that the way in which this happened was quite extraordinary.

Amazing recipe

Imagine if you took all the ingredients that make up a human being – carbon, hydrogen, oxygen and nitrogen – plus small amounts of a few other elements – principally sulphur, phosphorus, calcium and iron – and put them in a container with some water, gave it a vigorous stir and out stepped a completed person. That would be amazing!

Actually there's nothing terribly exotic in the chemicals that make us. If you wished to create another living object, whether it was a goldfish, a cucumber or a human being, you would really only need the principal elements mentioned before. Put these together in three dozen or so combinations to form some sugars, acids and other basic compounds, and you can build anything that lives.

Building blocks of life

In 1953, Stanley Miller, working at the University of Chicago, USA, took two flasks – one containing a little water to represent a primeval ocean, the other holding a mixture of methane, ammonia and hydrogen gases to represent the Earth's early atmosphere – connected them with rubber tubes and introduced some electrical sparks as a stand-in for lightning. After a few days, the water in the flasks had turned green and yellow in a thick broth of amino acids, fatty acids, sugars and other organic compounds. Amino acids, usually referred to as 'the building blocks of life', are the easy part of the recipe. The problem is proteins.

A little miracle

Proteins are what you get when you string amino acids together, and we need a lot of them. No one really knows, but there may be as many as a million types of protein in the human body, and each one is a tiny miracle because, by all the laws of probability, they shouldn't even exist.

To make a protein you need to assemble amino acids in a particular order, in much the same way that you assemble letters in a particular order to spell a word. The problem is that words in the amino-acid alphabet are often exceedingly long. For example, to spell 'collagen', the name of a common type of protein, you need to arrange eight letters in the right order. However, to **make** collagen, you need to arrange 1,055 amino acids in precisely the right sequence.

But – and here's the crucial point – you don't **make** it. It makes itself, spontaneously, without any help. So how's it done?

- To be of use, a protein must not only assemble amino acids in the right sequence . . .
- it must then engage in a kind of chemical origami and fold itself into a very specific shape.
- Then it must enlist the help of some DNA. Proteins can't exist without DNA and DNA is of no use to anybody without proteins.

And there's more still . . .

DNA, proteins and the other components of life couldn't go anywhere without some sort of cell to contain them. No atom or molecule has ever achieved life independently. Pluck any atom from your body and it's no more alive than a grain of sand. It's only when all the different materials come together within the shelter of a cell that life can occur.

An early start

One of the biggest surprises that geologists and other scientists have come up with in recent decades is just how early in Earth's history life arose. For a long time it was thought that life was less than 600 million years old. Thirty years ago, a few adventurous souls felt it went back 2.5 billion years. But the present date of 3.85 billion years is stunningly early.

The Earth's surface didn't become solid until about 3.9 billion years ago, so life got started pretty quickly. It's little wonder that we call it 'the miracle of life'.

Battling bacteria

At first there was no oxygen, just poisonous vapours from hydrochloric and sulphuric acids powerful enough to eat through clothing and blister skin.

Quite how anything survived on the planet billions of years ago is amazing. It certainly wouldn't have suited us. If you were to step from a time machine into that ancient world, you would very swiftly scamper back inside. The chemical stew that was the atmosphere then would have allowed hardly any sunlight to reach the Earth's surface. What little you could see would be lit up only briefly by frequent lightning flashes. In short, it was an Earth we wouldn't recognize.

For two billion years, bacterial organisms were the only forms of life. They lived, they reproduced, they swarmed, but they didn't show any particular inclination to move on to a more challenging level of existence. But then, at some point in the first billion years of life, blue-green bacterial algae, known as cyanobacteria, learned to tap into the hydrogen that is plentiful in water. They absorbed water molecules, supped on the hydrogen and released oxygen as waste.

Oxygen kills

That oxygen is poisonous often comes as a surprise to those of us who believe it's a friendly necessity. That's because we've evolved to exploit it. Our white blood cells use it to kill invading bacteria. However, to other things it's a terror. It's what turns butter rancid and makes iron rust.

However, even we can only tolerate it up to a point. The oxygen level in our cells is only about a tenth of the level found in the atmosphere.

Oxygen-makers

The cyanobacteria were a runaway success. As they spread, the world began to fill with oxygen. This didn't suit any of the other living organisms on the planet that found oxygen poisonous and they were soon vanquished, or else they took refuge in the oozy world of bogs and lake bottoms.

Life pops up

About 3.5 billion years ago something new started to happen. Wherever the seas were shallow, the cyanobacteria became very slightly tacky, and trapped micro-particles of dust and sand. They formed slightly weird but solid structures known as stromatolites. Sometimes these looked like enormous cauliflowers, sometimes like fluffy columns, rising tens of metres above the surface of the water.

Invasion of the mitochondria

One reason why life took so long to grow complex was that the world had to wait about two billion years for small organisms like the stromatolites to raise oxygen levels in the atmosphere to more or less current levels. But once the stage was set, an entirely new type of cell arose. Mitochondria are very tiny – you could pack a billion into the space occupied by a grain of sand – but also very hungry. Almost every nutriment you absorb goes to feeding them. We couldn't live for two minutes without them.

Millions of microbes

Eventually, there were many more kinds of these microbes – single-cell organisms that were too small to be seen by the human eye. They included bacteria and archaea (bacteria-like creatures that have different traits to true bacteria) and fungi. Then there were oxygen-makers like primitive algae, amoebas, slime moulds and protozoa. These were the microbes that learned to form into multicellular beings which would either expel oxygen – like plants – or take it in, like you and me. Finally, the viruses made up another major type of microbe.

Our oldest ancestors

For many years, scientists knew about stromatolites from fossils; but in 1961, they got a real surprise with the discovery of a community living on the remote northwest coast of Australia. Today, visitors can stroll over the water to get a good look at the stromatolites, quietly respiring just beneath the surface. They are dull and grey and look like very large cow-pats.

It's a curiously giddying moment to find yourself staring at living remnants of the Earth as it was 3.5 billion years ago.

It's worth remembering that the world, as we are about to see, still belongs to the very small.

Your mini world

Every human body consists of about ten quadrillion cells, but is host to about 100 quadrillion bacterial cells. They are, in short, a big part of us. From the bacteria's point of view, of course, we are a rather small part of them.

It's probably not a good idea to take too personal an interest in your microbes. At the same time, there's no point in trying to hide from them, for they are on and around you in numbers you can't conceive of. If you are in good health and averagely diligent about hygiene, you will have a herd of about one trillion bacteria grazing on your flesh – about 100,000 of them on every square centimetre of skin.

Bacteria buffet

They dine off the ten billion or so flakes of skin you shed every day, plus all the tasty oils and fortifying minerals that seep out from every pore and fissure. You are for them the ultimate buffet, with the convenience of warmth and constant mobility thrown in. By way of thanks, they give you body odour.

And those are just the bacteria that inhabit your skin. There are trillions more tucked away in your gut and nasal passages, clinging to your hair and eyelashes, swimming over the surface of your eyes, drilling through the enamel of your teeth. Your digestive system alone is host to more than 100 trillion microbes, of at least 400 types. Some deal with sugars, some with starches, some attack other bacteria. A surprising number have no apparent function at all. They just seem to like to be with you.

Standing together

We couldn't survive a day without our bacteria. They process our wastes and make them usable again; without their diligent munching nothing would rot. They purify our water and keep our soils productive. Bacteria synthesize vitamins in our gut, convert the things we eat into useful sugars and polysaccharides, and go to war on alien microbes that slip down our gullet. We depend totally on bacteria to pluck nitrogen from the air and convert it into useful nucleotides and amino acids for us. Above all, microbes continue to provide us with the air we breathe and to keep the atmosphere stable.

Never say die

Because we humans are big and clever enough to produce and use antibiotics and disinfectants, it's easy to convince ourselves that we can get rid of the bacteria we don't want. Don't you believe it!

Bacteria will eat wood, the glue in wallpaper, the metals in hardened paint. They have been found living in boiling mud pots and lakes of caustic soda, deep inside rocks, at the bottom of the sea, in hidden pools of icy water and under 11 kilometres of water pressure in the Pacific Ocean – the equivalent to being squashed beneath 50 jumbo jets.

Mooning around

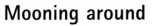

Perhaps the most extraordinary survival yet found was that of a streptococcus bacterium that was recovered from the sealed lens of a camera that had stood on the Moon for two years.

Bacteria will live and thrive on almost anything you spill, dribble or shake loose. After just 24 hours, bacteria are developing fast on this dish which has been coughed on. However, they have not grown on the antibiotic fluid in the centre.

There are few environments in which bacteria aren't prepared to live. They may not build cities or have interesting social lives, but they will be here until the universe finally ends.

Making you ill

So why, you are bound to ask at some point in your life, do microbes so often want to hurt us? What possible satisfaction could there be to a microbe in having us grow feverish or chilled, or disfigured with sores, or above all, dead? After all, if we're dead, we're hardly going to provide long-term hospitality.

Altogether, only about one microbe in 1,000 is infectious for humans – though we could be forgiven for thinking that that's quite enough. Microbes are still a top killer in the world.

To begin with, it's worth remembering that most microbes are harmless enough. Some are even beneficial to our health. The most infectious organism there is, a bacterium called Wolbachia, doesn't hurt humans at all – or, come to that, any other vertebrates. But if you are a shrimp or worm or fruit fly, it can make you wish you'd never been born.

Killer on the move

Making a host unwell has certain benefits for the microbe. Vomiting, sneezing and diarrhoea are excellent ways of getting out of one host and into position for boarding another. The microbe can also enlist the help of a mobile third party. Infectious organisms love mosquitoes because the mosquito's bite delivers them directly into a bloodstream where they can get straight to work before the victim's defence mechanisms can figure out what's hit them. This is why so many grade A diseases, such as malaria and yellow fever, begin with a mosquito bite.

In truth, micro-organisms don't care what they do to you any more than you care when you slaughter them by the millions with a spray of disinfectant. The only time your well-being is of consequence is when it kills you before it can move on; then it may well die out too.

The female mosquito sucks blood from other animals to nourish her eggs, passing on deadly diseases as she does.

To the rescue

Because there are so many things out there with the potential to hurt you, your body holds lots of different varieties of defensive white blood cells – some ten million types in all, each designed to identify and destroy a particular sort of invader. It would be impossible to keep ten million separate armies all at the ready, so each variety of white blood cell keeps just a few scouts on active duty. When an infectious agent invades, the relevant scouts identify the attacker and put out a call for reinforcements of the right type. While your body is manufacturing these forces, you are likely to feel wretched. But recovery begins when the troops swing into action.

White blood cells are merciless and will hunt down and kill every last invader they can find. To avoid extinction, attackers either strike quickly and move on to a new host, as with common infectious illnesses like flu, or they disguise themselves so that the white cells fail to spot them, as with HIV, the virus responsible for AIDS, which can sit harmlessly and unnoticed in the body's cells for years before springing into action.

Hijacker viruses

It may come as a slight comfort to know that bacteria can themselves get sick. They are sometimes infected by a virus. Smaller and simpler than bacteria, viruses aren't themselves alive. They hijack a suitable host and then use it to produce more virus.

Not being living organisms themselves, viruses can remain very simple. Many, including HIV, have ten genes or fewer, whereas even the simplest bacteria require several thousand. Viruses are also very tiny, much too small to be seen with a conventional microscope, but even so, they can do immense damage. Smallpox, in the twentieth century alone, killed an estimated 300 million people.

Some 5,000 species of virus are known, and between them they cause many hundreds of diseases, ranging from flu and the common cold to serious ones like smallpox, rabies, yellow fever, ebola, polio and AIDS.

And on that sobering note, it's time to leave the world of non-visible life.

113

So, here we are . . .

Geologists tried to make sense of the huge collection of fossils and rocks they'd been gathering from all over the world. There was some strange evidence that made no sense, but by solving its mystery, scientists would learn a great deal more about the inner workings of their planet.

What we know so far:

- We can trace back to a time when the world's tectonic plates were fused into one huge shape we call Pangaea.
- Our planet is a hot ball of molten rock with cooler layers and a hard crust.
- The oceans and atmosphere that surround us help maintain Earth's temperature.
- Water and gases on our early planet allowed microscopic life to emerge.
- Microbes and bacteria are the most numerous and successful living things on the planet.

What happens above and below the Earth's crust?

1908 Frank Bursley Taylor suggests that the Earth's continents had once slid around, and that this same shifting produced mountain chains.

1912 Alfred Wegener examines the movements of trilobites and suggests that the continents might have shifted over huge spans of time.

1935 American geologists Beno Gutenberg and Charles Richter come up with the Richter scale, a way of measuring the strength of earthquakes.

1950s Eugene Shoemaker begins his important research on the impact of asteroids on Earth's surface.

1963 Matthews and Vine find evidence of ocean-floor spreading, and confirm the movement of continents, or plate tectonics.

1970s Walter Alvarez and his father announce they have discovered evidence of an asteroid impact that just might have been the one that eliminated dinosaurs from the face of the Earth.

Danger zones

We have visited precarious sites all over the planet:
the Lisbon earthquake of 1755; Tokyo, perched on
the edge of three moving plates; Mount St Helens,
a surprise volcanic eruption;
Yellowstone Park with its
bubbling warnings; the huge
crater left in Manson, Iowa;
the Mariana Trench 11
kilometres below the sea; and
the approaching asteroid
Apophis, which
has yet to give us
a fright in 2029.

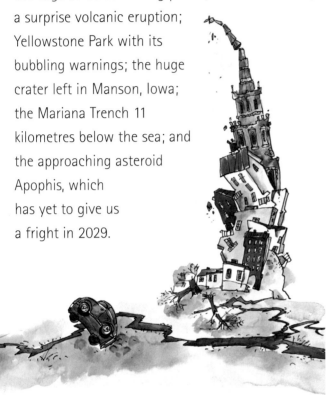

We are forced to conclude that with volcanoes and
earthquakes rattling the surface and asteroids lunging
at us from outer space, we're very lucky to live as
quietly as we do.

Our small spot

We also discovered that we only occupy half a per
cent of the planet's surface since the rest is too
watery, rocky, high, low, hot, or cold to live on.

We examined the air above and the ocean depths
below and discovered that we are subjected to
huge pressure in both places.

We found out that tiny bacterial organisms are a
lot hardier than we are. This is how they managed
to survive on a harsh planet billions of years ago.

And we know that these same bacterial forms
thrive today – many of them on us!

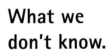

What we don't know.

Quite how the bacteria
that emerged from the
warm seas of long ago
became the tall, masterful
and clever beings that are
us, is a miraculous story
waiting to unfold.

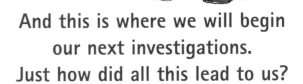

And this is where we will begin
our next investigations.
Just how did all this lead to us?

Citizen cells

It starts with a single cell. This splits to become two, and the two become four, and so on. After just 47 doublings, you have 140 trillion cells in your body and are ready to spring forth as a human being.

It's been estimated that you lose 500 brain cells an hour. So if you have any serious thinking to do, there really isn't a moment to waste.

A thing of wonder

To build the most basic yeast cell, you would have to miniaturize about the same number of components as are found in a Boeing 777 jetliner and fit them into a sphere just five microns across. But yeast cells are as nothing compared to the complexity of human cells.

You have no secrets from your cells. They know far more about you than you do. Each carries a copy of the instruction manual for your body and knows how to do not only its own job, but every other job too. Your cells are a country of 10,000 trillion citizens and there isn't a thing they don't do for you. They let you feel pleasure and form thoughts. They enable you to stand, stretch and leap about. When you eat, they extract the nutrients, distribute the energy, and carry off the waste – they also remember to make you hungry in the first place and make you feel good afterwards so you won't forget to eat again. They keep your hair growing, your ears waxed, your brain purring. They will jump to your defence the instant you are threatened, and die unhesitatingly for you – billions of them do so daily.

Here today, gone tomorrow

Most living cells seldom last more than a month or so, but there are some notable exceptions. Brain cells last as long as you do. You are issued with 100 billion or so at birth and that's all you're ever going to get. The good news is that the parts that make up your brain cells are constantly renewed. In fact, it's been suggested that there isn't a single bit of any of us – not so much as a stray molecule – that was part of us nine years ago.

Frenzied world

If you could visit a cell, you wouldn't like it. Blown up to a scale at which atoms are about the size of peas, a cell itself would be a sphere roughly 800 metres across, and supported by a complex framework of girders called the cytoskeleton. Within it, millions upon millions of objects – some the size of basketballs, others the size of cars – would whizz about like bullets. There wouldn't be a place you could stand without being pummelled and ripped thousands of times every second from every direction.

Nearly all your cells are built to the same plan: they have an outer casing or membrane, a nucleus holding the necessary information to keep you going, and a busy space between the two called the cytoplasm.

Your battery

It's a molecule called adenosine triphosphate, or ATP for short, that keeps you going. ATP molecules are little battery packs that provide energy for all the cell's processes, and you get through a lot of them. At any given moment, a typical cell in your body will have about one billion ATP molecules in it, and in two minutes every one of them will have been drained dry and another billion will have taken their place. Feel the warmth of your skin. That's your ATP at work.

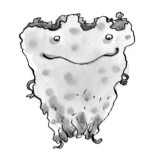

Break up the cells of a sponge by passing it through a sieve, then dump the bits in a solution and they will build themselves into a sponge again.

You can do this to them over and over again, and they will doggedly reassemble . . .

Like you and me and every other living thing, they have one overwhelming impulse: to continue to exist.

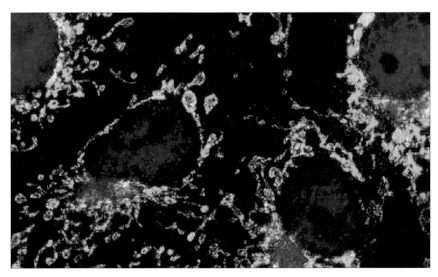

Energy production of a cell.

How long can you stay?

It is a curious feature of our existence that we come from a planet that is very good at promoting life but even better at extinguishing it. The average species on Earth lasts for only about four million years.

It's worth remembering that the human species has already been around for roughly two million years.

Be prepared to change

If you wish to be around for billions of years, you must be prepared to change everything about yourself – your shape, size, colour, species affiliation, everything – and you will need to do so repeatedly. Of course that's much easier said than done. To get from a single-celled blob of protoplasm to a thinking, feeling, upright modern human being has required you to take on new traits over and over in a precisely timely manner for an exceedingly long while.

So at various periods over the last 3.8 billion years you have:

- shunned oxygen and then doted on it,
- grown fins and limbs and jaunty sails,
- laid eggs,
- flicked the air with a forked tongue,
- been sleek,
  - been furry,
    - lived underground,
      - lived in trees,
        - been as big as a deer
          - and as small as a mouse, and a million things more.

Count yourself lucky

The tiniest deviation from any of these evolutionary stages and you might now be licking algae from cave walls, or lolling walrus-like on some stony shore, or disgorging air through a blowhole in the top of your head before diving down for a mouthful of delicious sandworms.

Not one of our key ancestors was:

squashed

drowned

devoured

stuck fast

starved

mortally wounded

or otherwise prevented from its life's purpose of delivering a tiny spurt of life-making material to the right partner at the right moment.

Not only have you been lucky enough to be attached since time immemorial to a favoured evolutionary line, but you have also been extremely – make that miraculously – fortunate in your personal ancestry. Consider the fact that for 3.8 billion years, a period of time older than the Earth's mountains and rivers and oceans, every one of your forebears, on both sides, has been attractive enough to find a mate, healthy enough to reproduce, and sufficiently blessed by fate and circumstances to live long enough to do so. This would keep going the one and only possible sequence of hereditary combinations that would result eventually in you.

Let's try, as best we can, to understand exactly how all this change came about.

A runaway success

Trilobites first appeared about 540 million years ago, near what was thought to be the start of the great burst of complex, or multi-cell, life known as the Cambrian explosion. They then vanished, along with a great deal else, in the mysterious Permian extinction. But although they became extinct, they were among the most successful animals ever to live.

Compared to the trilobite, humans have so far survived for one-half of 1 per cent as long.

In no rush

Trilobites reigned for 300 million years – twice as long as the dinosaurs, who were also among history's great survivors. Over this huge amount of time, the trilobites rapidly evolved into new forms. Most remained small, about the size of modern beetles, and grew nervous systems, probing antennae, a brain of sorts, and eyes. There was not just one adventurous species but at least 60,000 – and they didn't appear in one or two locations, but all over the globe.

Teeming trilobites

In 1909, while climbing on a mountain trail high up in the Canadian Rockies, the American palaeontologist Charles Doolittle Walcott came across a layer of sedimentary rock containing an unmatched collection of fossils. The outcrop, known as the Burgess Shale, was formed 500 million years ago when the area wasn't at the top of a mountain at all but at the foot of one. It lay in a shallow ocean basin at the bottom of a steep cliff. The seas at that time teemed with life, but normally the animals left no record because they were soft-bodied and decayed when they died. Here, however, the cliff had collapsed and the creatures below were pressed into the mudslide like flowers in a book, their features preserved in wonderful detail.

Ancient arthopods

During annual summer trips up to 1925, Walcott excavated tens of thousands of specimens into a unique collection. Some of the fossils had shells; many others did not. Some of the creatures were sighted; others blind. The variety was enormous, consisting of 140 species by one count. Walcott became a leading authority on trilobites and was the first person to establish that they were arthropods, the group that includes modern insects and crustaceans.

It isn't easy to become a fossil

The fate of nearly all living organisms is to slowly rot away to nothing. Only about one bone in a billion, and less than one species in 120,000, has made it into the fossil record. What we have is the tiniest sample of all the life that the Earth has spawned. And about 95 per cent of it is of animals that once lived under water, not land ones. The chances of becoming a fossil are very small.

• First, you must die in the right place. Only about 15 per cent of rocks can preserve fossils, so it's no good keeling over where you'll be melted into volcanic granite.

• Next you must become buried in sediment where you can leave an impression, like a leaf in wet mud.
• You must also rot without exposure to oxygen, so the molecules in your bones and hard parts are replaced by dissolved minerals, creating a petrified copy of the original.

• Then, as the sediments in which your fossil lies are pushed about by Earth's processes, it must somehow maintain its shape.
• Finally, but above all, after tens of millions of years of being hidden away, your fossil must be found and recognized as something worth keeping.

Detail of a fossil fern embedded in rock.

Time to get started

Life is an odd thing. It seems it couldn't wait to get going, but having done so, it was then in very little hurry to move on. If you compress the 4,500 million years of Earth's history into a normal 24-hour day, then single-cell organisms came to life very early, about 4 a.m. But then, everything stands still for the next 16 hours.

Life's 24-hour day

The planet is formed at 1 a.m., but this is a hot, poisonous place where life can't get started. Then, around 4 a.m. the earliest life forms emerge.

Not until almost 8.30 p.m. has the Earth anything to show but a restless skin of microbes.

At 9.04 p.m. trilobites swim onto the scene, followed by the shapely creatures of the Burgess Shale. Then the first sea plants appear, followed 20 minutes later by the first jellyfish and early lichens.

Just before 10 p.m. plants begin to pop up on the land. Soon after, with less than two hours left in the day, the first land creatures follow. Thanks to ten minutes or so of balmy weather, by 10.24 the Earth is covered in the great carboniferous forests whose residues give us all our coal, and the first winged insects are evident.

Dinosaurs plod onto the scene just before 11 p.m. and hold sway for about three-quarters of an hour.

At 21 minutes to midnight they vanish and the age of mammals begins. Humans emerge 1 minute and 17 seconds before midnight.

The whole of our recorded history, on this scale, would be no more than a few seconds; a single human lifetime would be barely an instant.

122

Waiting in the wings

Just as mammals bided their time for 100 million years until the dinosaurs cleared off, and then seemingly burst forth all over the planet, so too perhaps the arthropods and later creatures waited in semi-microscopic anonymity for the soft-bodied organisms found by fossil-hunters to have their day.

The will to live

Consider the lichen. If we were told we had to spend decades becoming a furry growth on a rock, we would probably lose the will to live. Lichens clearly don't. They're just about the hardiest visible organisms on Earth. They thrive in a sunny spot and also where there is little competition from other, faster-growing plants. Therefore, in Antarctica, where virtually nothing else will grow, you can find vast expanses of them – 400 types in all – clinging devotedly to every wind-whipped rock.

Because lichens grow on bare rock without any obvious food source and without producing seeds, people at first believed they were stones. Closer inspection showed they were a clever mix of half fungi and half algae. The fungi excrete acids which dissolve the surface of the rock, freeing minerals that the algae convert into food for them both.

Human reach

Perhaps an even better way of understanding just how recently we arrived in this 4.5-billion-year-old picture is to stretch your arms to their fullest extent and imagine that width as the entire history of the Earth.

On this scale, the distance from the fingertips of one hand to the wrist of the other is Precambrian. All of complex life is in one hand, and in a single stroke with a medium-grained nail file you could eradicate human history.

Out of the sea

As we have seen, any time that life does something bold it's quite an event – and few occasions were more eventful than when life moved on a stage and came out of the sea.

Out of the frying pan . . .

There was a powerful incentive to leave the water: it was getting dangerous down there. The slow fusion of the continents into a single land mass, Pangaea, meant there was much less coastline than before and thus less coastal habitat. So competition was fierce. There was also an omnivorous and unsettling new type of predator on the scene, one so perfectly designed for attack that it has scarcely changed since it first appeared: the shark.

. . . into the fire

Land was a formidable environment: hot, dry, bathed in intense ultraviolet radiation and difficult to move on. To live on land, creatures had to undergo wholesale revisions of their anatomies. Hold a fish at each end and it sags in the middle, its backbone too weak to support it. To survive out of water, marine creatures needed a stronger load-bearing bone structure. Above all, any land creature would have to develop a way to take its oxygen directly from the air rather than filter it from water. None of these were things that could happen overnight, but happen they did.

The first visible mobile residents on dry land were probably like modern woodlice. These are the little bugs (crustaceans, in fact) that are commonly thrown into confusion when you upturn a rock or log.

Plants began the process of land colonization about 450 million years ago, accompanied of necessity by tiny mites and other organisms which they needed to break down and recycle dead organic matter on their behalf.

Larger animals took a little longer to emerge.

Before 400 million years ago, nothing walked on land. After that time lots of things did.

Breathe in

For those that learned to breathe oxygen from the air, times were good. Oxygen levels in the early periods when terrestrial life first blossomed may have been as high as 35 per cent (it's nearer 20 per cent now). This allowed animals to grow remarkably large remarkably quickly. The oldest indication of a land animal yet found is a track left 350 million years ago by a millipede-like creature on a rock in Scotland. It was over a metre long. Before the era was out, some millipedes would reach lengths more than double that.

The principal reason oxygen levels were high was that much of the world's landscape was dominated by giant tree ferns and vast swamps. Instead of completely rotting away, dead vegetation settled in rich, wet sediments, which were eventually squeezed into vast coal beds.

Airborne

With huge creatures on the prowl, it is perhaps not surprising that insects in this period evolved a trick that could keep them safely out of tongueshot: they learned to fly. Some took to this new means of locomotion with such uncanny facility that they haven't changed their techniques in all the time since.

Dragonflies grew as big as ravens. Then, as now, dragonflies could cruise at over 50 kilometres an hour, instantly stop, hover, fly backwards, and lift far more – proportionate to their size – than any flying machine humans have come up with.

Trees and other vegetation grew to outsized proportions. Horsetail and tree ferns reached heights of 15 metres, club mosses 40 metres.

Where did we come from?

The first land animals from which we came are something of a mystery. Many animals are tetrapods – they have four limbs, each of which ends in a maximum of five fingers or toes. Dinosaurs, whales, birds, humans – even fish – are all tetrapods, which clearly suggests they come from a single common ancestor. However, no fossils have been found that conclusively link fish with land creatures.

We almost certainly don't owe our existence to a fish that decided to sprout legs and walk out of the sea.

Life on land

There were four main branches of early reptilian life. One was wiped out early on, while another gave rise to the turtles and a third evolved into dinosaurs. The last sometimes looked like dinosaurs but were actually reptiles and it was a later branch of these that developed into mammals proper – and us.

Waiting our turn

It wasn't all plain sailing, however. Unfortunately for this last group, their cousins the dinosaurs proved too much to cope with. Unable to compete head-to-head with them, our ancestors by and large vanished from the record. However, a very few evolved into small, furry, burrowing beings that bided their time for a very long while as little mammals. The biggest of them grew no larger than a housecat, and most were no bigger than mice. One, a mouse-like animal, hadrocodium, had a tiny body weighing just two grammes – the same as a paper clip – but had a brain that, compared to other mammals, was very big for its size. Eventually, their small size would prove their salvation, but they would have to wait nearly 150 million years for the Age of Dinosaurs to come to an abrupt end.

Great survivors

We don't really know a great deal about the dinosaurs, as fewer than 1,000 species have been identified. They ruled the Earth for roughly three times as long as mammals and remained numerous until one single event wiped them out.

Going, going, gone

No one knows how many species of organisms have existed since life began: 30 billion is a commonly used figure, but the number has been put as high as 4,000 billion. Whatever the actual total, 99.99 per cent of all species that have ever lived are no longer with us.

Each of these huge transformations was dependent on that improbable driving force of progress: extinction.

Dinosaur trackway site with exposed fossil tracks of lower Jurassic age.

Comings and goings

The Earth has seen five major extinction episodes in its time. The Ordovician and Devonian each wiped out about 80 to 85 per cent of species. The Triassic and Cretaceous wiped out 70 to 75 per cent of species.

The 'whopper' extinction

But the real whopper was the Permian mass extinction, which raised the curtain on the dinosaurs. In the Permian, at least 95 per cent of animals known from the fossil record checked out, never to return. Trilobites vanished altogether. Clams and sea urchins nearly went. Even about a third of insect species went.

What was that?

In nearly every case, for both big and small extinctions, we have little idea of the main cause. It could have been global warming, or even global cooling, changing sea levels, loss of oxygen from the seas, epidemics, giant leaks of methane gas from the sea floor, meteor and comet impacts, runaway hurricanes, solar flares or volcanic upheavals. Furthermore, scientists can't agree whether certain extinctions happened over millions or thousands of years, or simply in one lively day.

Key extinction losses

Ordovician (440 million years ago) – conodonts went along with some trilobites.

Devonian (365 million years ago) – placoderms, heavily armoured jawed fish, lost.

Permian (245 million years ago) – pelycosaurs gone.

Triassic (210 million years ago) - almost all marine reptiles die out.

Cretaceous (65 million yars ago) - tyrannosaurus becomes extinct.

The KT extinction

Why, out of all the thousands of meteor impacts Earth has endured, was the event of 65 million years ago, the one we call the KT event, so devastating? First, it was positively enormous. It struck with the force of 100 million megatonnes – that's more than one Hiroshima-sized bomb for every person alive today. And why did the event wipe out every single dinosaur while other reptiles, like snakes and crocodiles, survived? Clearly, it helped to live in water, which offered protection against heat and flame. All the land-based animals that survived had a habit of retreating to safety, either in water or underground, and, on the whole, the big animals were wiped out while the small, furtive ones survived.

Mega mammals and big birds

With the dinosaurs gone, the mammals expanded wildly. For a time, there were guinea pigs the size of rhinos, and rhinos the size of a two-storey house. The gigantic, flightless, carnivorous titanis was the most daunting bird that ever lived. It stood over two metres high, weighed up to 150 kilograms and had a beak that could tear the head off pretty much anything that annoyed it.

Horse-less

In between the big kill-offs, there have also been many smaller, less well-known extinctions which often hit particular populations. Grazing animals, for example, including horses, were nearly wiped out about five million years ago.

We've found out three things about life:

- it has a powerful will to exist;
- it doesn't always want much;
- it will from time to time become extinct.

To this we may add a fourth: life goes on, often in ways that are decidedly amazing.

Labelling life

As Victorian collectors gathered up their samples of amazing fauna and flora from all over the world, all this new information needed to be filed, ordered and compared with what was known. The world was desperate for a workable system that sorted and named everything – a system of classification. Yet one had been available for about a century.

Rosa sylvestris alba cum rubore, folio glabro.

Rosa canina.

A rose by any other name

In the early 1730s, the Swedish botanist Carolus Linnaeus began to produce catalogues of the world's plant and animal species using a system he devised himself, and gradually his fame grew. Before this, plants were given names that were long-winded and elaborate. The common ground cherry was called *Physalis amno ramosissime ramis angulosis glabris foliis dentoserratis*. Linnaeus lopped it back to *Physalis angulata*. Then there were inconsistencies of naming. A botanist could not be sure if *Rosa sylvestris alba cum rubore, folio glabro* was the same plant that others called *Rosa sylvestris inodora seu canina*. Linnaeus solved the puzzlement by calling it simply *Rosa canina*. In a nutshell, he had given each species a two-word name: a surname, or family name, and a first, or special name.

All in order

The Linnaean system is so well established that it's difficult to imagine an alternative, but, before Linnaeus, systems of classification were often highly whimsical. Animals might be categorized by whether they were wild or domesticated, terrestrial or aquatic, large or small, even by whether they were thought handsome and noble or of no consequence. Linnaeus made it his life's work to put this right by classifying every living thing according to its physical attributes. Taxonomy – which is to say the science of classification – has never looked back.

When is a whale . . . ?

In the beginning, Linnaeus intended to give each plant only a genus name and a number – Brown beetle 1, Brown beetle 2, and so on. However, he soon realized that this was unsatisfactory. In the end, he named some 13,000 species of plant and animal; but what was special about his system was its consistency, order, simplicity and timeliness. He saw that whales belonged with cows, mice and other common terrestrial animals in the order Quadrupedia (later changed to Mammalia), which no one had done before.

Plants and animals

Originally, Linnaeus had three kingdoms in his scheme, namely Plants, Animals and Minerals (which has long since been abandoned). The animal world was divided into six categories: mammals, reptiles, birds, fishes, insects, and 'vermes', or worms (into which category he put everything that didn't fit into the first five). Since Linnaeus, scientists have added three new kingdoms: monera, for forms like bacteria; protista for protozoans and most algae; and fungi.

Your labels

Linnaeus recorded every living thing from its species name down to its primitive domain origins. You are from:

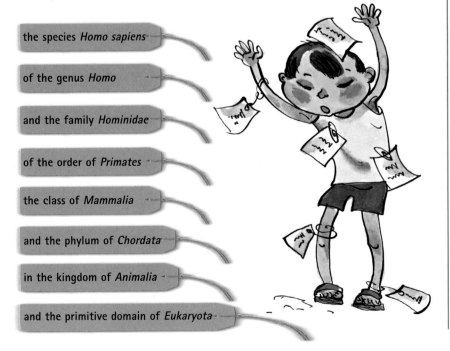

- the species *Homo sapiens*
- of the genus *Homo*
- and the family *Hominidae*
- of the order of *Primates*
- the class of *Mammalia*
- and the phylum of *Chordata*
- in the kingdom of *Animalia*
- and the primitive domain of *Eukaryota*

A name for himself

Rarely has a man been more comfortable with his own greatness than Linnaeus. He declared that there had never been 'a greater botanist or zoologist', and that his system of classification was 'the greatest achievement in the realm of science'. Modestly, he suggested that his gravestone should bear the inscription *Princeps Botanicorum*, 'Prince of Botanists'. It was never wise to question him on this. Those who did so were apt to find they had a kind of weed named after them.

Can't count?

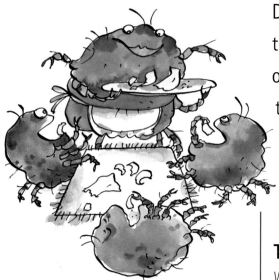

Despite Linnaeus's admirable work, we don't have the faintest idea of the number of things that live on our planet. Estimates range from three million to 200 million species, but it's possible that as many as 97 per cent of the world's plant and animal species may still await discovery. Why is this?

What a handful!

Go out into the woods – any woods at all – bend down and scoop up a handful of soil, and you will be holding up to ten billion bacteria, most of them unknown to science.

Your sample will also contain perhaps a million plump yeasts, some 200,000 hairy little fungi known as moulds, perhaps 10,000 protozoans (of which the most familiar is the amoeba), and assorted flatworms, roundworms and other microscopic creatures known collectively as cryptozoa. A large portion of these will also be unknown.

Too small

We have already established that most of the living things on the planet are microscopic. This may not be such a bad thing. You might not sleep nearly so well if you were aware that your mattress is home to perhaps two million microscopic mites, which come out in the wee hours to sup on your oily flesh and feast on all those crunchy flakes of skin that you shed as you doze. Your pillow alone may be home to 40,000 of them. Indeed, if your pillow is six years old, it's been estimated that one tenth of its weight will be made up of 'sloughed skin, living mites, dead mites and mite dung'. (But at least they're *your* mites!)

Too remote

It's likely that we haven't found a great many species simply because we're not looking in the right places. One botanist spent a few days tramping around a small patch of jungle in Borneo and discovered a thousand new species of flowering plant – more than exist in the whole of North America. The plants weren't hard to find, it's just that no one had looked there before. Tropical rainforests cover only about 6 per cent of Earth's surface, but they hold more than half of its animal life and about two-thirds of its flowering plants – and most of this forested area remains unknown.

Too few people looking

The stock of things to be found, examined and recorded far exceeds the number of scientists available to do it. Take the little-known organisms called bdelloid rotifers. These are microscopic animals that can survive almost anything. When conditions are tough, they curl up in a ball, switch off their metabolism and wait for better times. You can drop them into boiling water or freeze them almost to absolute zero, yet, when this torment has finished, they will uncurl and move on as if nothing had happened. So far, about 500 species of bdelloid rotifer have been identified, but nobody has any idea how many there may be altogether – probably because you could count the people who are even faintly interested on one hand.

Too much space to look in

The okapi, the nearest living relative of the giraffe, is now known to exist in substantial numbers in the rainforests of Zaire in Africa – the total population is estimated at perhaps 30,000. Yet its existence wasn't even suspected in the Western world until the 1900s, although an image of one was carved onto the wall of a building at Persepolis, in ancient Persia, in about 480 B.C. The large, flightless New Zealand bird called the takahe had been presumed extinct for 200 years before it was found very much alive in a rugged area of South Island. In 1995, a team of French and British scientists in Tibet, who were lost in a snowstorm in a remote valley, came across a breed of horse called the riwoche that had previously been known only from prehistoric cave drawings.

Lost centipedes

In the 1980s, amateur cave explorers entered a deep cave in Romania that had been sealed off from the outside world for a long but unknown period and found 33 species of insects and other small creatures – spiders, centipedes, lice – all blind, colourless and new to science. They were living off the microbes in the surface scum of pools and hot springs.

We may feel frustrated at the impossibility of tracking everything down but it's also unbearably exciting. We live on a planet that has an endless capacity to surprise us.

Journey to the future

In the middle 1800s, the naturalist Charles Darwin had what has been called 'the single best idea anyone has ever had' – and then locked it away in a drawer for the next 15 years.

Chance of a lifetime

Charles Darwin was destined for a career in the church; then, out of the blue, came a more tempting offer. He was invited to sail on the naval survey ship HMS *Beagle*, whose assignment was to chart coastal waters around South America. In every respect, the *Beagle* voyage was a triumph. Darwin experienced adventure enough to last a lifetime and collected a hoard of specimens sufficient to make his reputation and keep him occupied for years. He found a magnificent trove of giant ancient fossils, including the finest megatherium – a sort of giant ground sloth – known to date; survived a lethal earthquake in Chile; discovered a new species of dolphin; made useful geological investigations throughout the Andes; and developed a much-admired theory about the formation of coral reefs.

Life's a struggle

Aged 27, he returned home to reflect on what he'd seen; the idea came to him that life for most species is a perpetual struggle to survive. It was clear that some prospered and passed on that advantage to their offspring. In this way, certain species were continuously improving while others were failing and dying out. The idea took some time to come together. Because of the need to sort through crates and crates of *Beagle* specimens, it wasn't until 1842, five years after his return to England, that Darwin finally began to sketch out his new theory.

Man and ape

The one thing everyone thinks was the centre of Darwin's argument – that humans are descended from apes – didn't feature in it at all, except as a passing mention. Even so, Darwin was careful to keep his entire theory to himself because he well knew the storm it would cause. In fact, his manuscript might have remained locked away until his death had it not been for the arrival of a letter from a young naturalist named Alfred Russel Wallace, outlining a theory of natural selection that was uncannily similar to Darwin's secret jottings.

Wallace and Darwin had been corresponding for some time, and Wallace had more than once generously sent Darwin specimens he thought might interest him. Of course, Wallace had no idea that the theory he was about to publish was almost identical to one that Darwin had been evolving for two decades.

On the Origin of Species

Darwin was forced to publish his own work early, and on 1 July 1858, both Darwin's and Wallace's theories were unveiled to the world. Darwin's suggested a mechanism for how a species might become stronger or better – in a word, fitter. As anticipated, it upset many people, particularly those who believed that religious stories explained Man's origins.

Much later, Darwin did publish his belief that humans are related to the apes in *The Descent of Man*. The conclusion was a bold one, since nothing in the fossil record supported such an idea. The only known early human remains of that time were a famous discovery of Neanderthal bones in Germany and a few uncertain fragments of jawbones from elsewhere. *The Descent of Man* was altogether a more controversial book than the *Origin*, but by the time it appeared, the world had grown less excitable and its arguments caused less of a stir.

The scientific world was, it seemed, ready to acknowledge where we came from – but still didn't have any explanation for how. They were about to learn.

The quiet monk

Mendel chose peas because they reproduce quickly. They also have something called simple traits – characteristics that were easy to spot – colour, shape, and so on.

Darwin believed that any strong trait that arose in one generation of a species would be passed on to subsequent generations and, in time, would strengthen the species. However, some argued that the trait would become diluted and weaker as it was passed on. Unknown to Darwin, in a quiet corner of central Europe, a retiring monk named Gregor Mendel was about to come up with proof that he was right.

Mendel was born in 1822 to a humble farming family in what is now the Czech Republic. A monk with a strong interest in gardening, he was also a trained scientist – he had studied physics and mathematics, and he brought scientific discipline to all he did. Moreover, the monastery at Brno was known as a learned institution. It had a library of 20,000 books and a strong scientific tradition.

A greenhouse lab

Before embarking on his experiments, Mendel spent two years preparing his control specimens, seven varieties of pea, to make sure they bred true. Then, helped by two full-time assistants, he repeatedly bred and cross-bred hybrids from 30,000 pea plants. It was delicate work. They had to avoid accidental cross-fertilization and note every slight variation in the growth and appearance of seeds, pods, leaves, stems and flowers.

Like peas in a pod

He established that every seed contained two 'factors', one from each parent pea – a dominant one and a recessive one – and that when these combined, they produced predictable patterns of inheritance. Today we know that Mendel's work laid the basis for our present understanding of genes – the parts of our chromosomes that make us both the same as and different from each other. He discovered the secret of hereditary traits, the reason we are like our parents: why we are tall, short, fat, thin and indeed, often enjoy a strong resemblance to the rest of our family. He never used the word 'gene' since it didn't exist then; but it was, in effect, the science of genetics that he invented.

Back to the birds and bees

Altogether, Mendel spent eight years on the peas, then confirmed his results with experiments on flowers, corn and other plants. If anything, he was too scientific in his approach. When he presented his findings at a meeting of the Natural History Society of Brno in 1865, the audience of about 40 listened politely but weren't at all enthusiastic. Equally, the great botanists of the time failed to see that Mendel had made a breakthrough in explaining why we are what we are. Frustrated, the monk retired to his monastery, where he became abbot and grew exceptional vegetables while studying bees, mice and sunspots, among a great deal else.

Two great men

Mendel's studies were all but lost until they were rediscovered by scientists in 1900 and, in time, the world started to give them the recognition they deserved. Darwin saw that all living things are connected and ultimately traced their ancestry to a single, common source; Mendel's work provided the understanding of inheritance that supported this. Together, without realizing it, they had laid the groundwork for all life sciences in the 20th century.

However, it is fairly amazing to reflect that, a hundred years ago, the best scientific minds couldn't actually tell you where babies came from. Let's find out.

One big happy family

If your two parents hadn't bonded just when they did – possibly to the second, even to the nanosecond – you wouldn't be here. And if their parents hadn't bonded in precisely the same exacting manner, you wouldn't be here either. And if their parents hadn't done likewise, and their parents before them, and so on, obviously and indefinitely, you wouldn't be here.

We are all uncannily alike. Compare your genes with any other human being's and, on average, they will be about 99.9 per cent the same. That is what makes us a species.

Dear Uncle William . . .

Push backwards through time and these ancestral debts begin to add up. Go back just eight generations to about the time that Charles Darwin and Abraham Lincoln were born, and already there are over 250 people on whose couplings your existence depends. Continue further, to the time of Shakespeare, and you have no fewer than 16,384 ancestors. If you go back 20 generations in your family, the number of people who have had children on your behalf is 1,048,576. Five generations further back it would add up to 33,554,432, and so on. You can begin to see what a lot of energy has gone into making you.

However, with so many millions of ancestors in your background, there will have been many occasions when a relative from your mother's side of the family procreated with some distant cousin from your father's side. Indeed, if you look around you on a bus or in a park or café or any crowded place, most of the people you see are very probably relatives.

In the most fundamental sense, we are all family.

138

The eye of a fly

It was an American scientist, Thomas Hunt Morgan, who proved that it was the chromosomes in cells that were at the heart of inherited traits. In 1908 Morgan began to study the tiny, delicate fruit fly.

As laboratory specimens, fruit flies have certain advantages: they cost almost nothing to house and feed, can be bred by the millions in milk bottles, go from egg to productive parenthood in ten days or less and have just four pairs of chromosomes, which keeps things simple.

Morgan and his team meticulously bred and cross-bred millions of flies, each of which was captured with tweezers and examined for any tiny inherited differences. For six years they tried to produce a change in the breed by zapping the flies with X-rays, rearing them in bright light or darkness, baking them gently in ovens, spinning them crazily – but nothing worked. Morgan was on the brink of giving up when a fly emerged that had white eyes rather than the usual red ones. Now he was able to reproduce the trait in successive generations and prove that chromosomes were at the heart of inheritance.

Unravelling the chain

Each of your 10,000 trillion cells has a nucleus. Inside each nucleus are 46 chromosomes, of which 23 come from your mother and 23 from your father. Inside each chromosome are threadlike particles made of a wonder chemical called deoxyribonucleic acid or DNA. Ninety-seven per cent of your DNA consists of nothing but long stretches of meaningless garble. Only here and there along each strand do you find sections that control vital functions. These are the long-elusive genes.

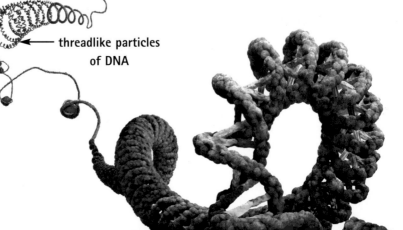

nucleus

chromosomes

threadlike particles of DNA

Peel back the skin ...

Over 60 per cent of human genes are the same as those of the fruit fly. We are quite closely related to fruit and vegetables too. For example, about half the chemical functions that take place in a banana are the same as those that take place in you.

We have 20,000-25,000 genes, about the same number as are found in grass. Clearly it's not the number you have that matters, but what you do with them.

Chain of life

By playing with pieces of cardboard cut into the shapes of the four chemical components that make up DNA, two scientists called Francis Crick and James Watson were able to work out how the pieces fitted together in pairs. From this discovery in 1953 it only took them a day or two to make a Meccano-like model – perhaps the most famous in modern science – consisting of metal plates bolted together in a spiral. It was without question a brilliant piece of detective work, for which they were awarded the Nobel Prize.

The double helix

A secret code

Crick and Watson decided that if you could find out the shape of a DNA molecule you'd be able to see how it did what it did. The shape, as everyone now knows, is rather like a spiral staircase: the famous double helix. DNA is actually very simple. It has just four basic components – which is like having an alphabet of just four letters.

The components pair up in particular ways to form the 'rungs', and the order in which they do this as you move up or down the ladder forms the DNA code. Because you can combine them in different ways, like you do with the simple dots and dashes of the Morse code, you end up with 3.2 billion letters of coding, enough to provide a number of possible combinations that is almost impossible to imagine. ($10^{1,920,000,000}$, if you really want to know.)

Long-life evidence

DNA is not itself alive. No molecule is, but DNA is especially 'unalive'. That's why it can be recovered from patches of long-dried blood in murder investigations, and coaxed from ancient bones to date prehistoric people.

DNA to protein

Although the existence of large amounts of DNA in each human cell was discovered over a hundred years back, it was thought it didn't *do* much at all. Later, DNA was linked to the making of proteins, a process vital to life. But as proteins are made *outside* the nucleus of cells, no one could work out how the DNA could be getting messages out to them.

The answer, we now know, is ribonucleic acid, or RNA, which acts as an interpreter between the two. DNA and proteins don't speak the same language; it's as if one spoke Hindi and the other Spanish. To communicate, they need a mediator in the form of RNA. Working with a kind of chemical clerk called a ribosome, RNA translates information from a cell's DNA into terms proteins can understand and act upon.

DNA exists for just one reason: to create more DNA – and you have a lot of it inside you: nearly two metres squeezed into almost every cell. In fact, you may contain as much as 20 billion kilometres of DNA.

Now let's leave the world of what we're made of, and look at where we began.

Hot and cold

As we have seen, we need a certain type of climate – not too hot and not too cold – in order to survive. As the Earth moves through space, its tilt and orbit around the Sun changes. This affects the strength of sunlight falling on different parts of Earth at any one time and brings about hot and cold spells.

Climate and the caretaker

We owe this knowledge not to some learned scientist but to a humble caretaker. Born in 1821, James Croll worked at a variety of jobs – carpenter, insurance salesman, hotel manager – before becoming a janitor at a university in Glasgow, Scotland. There he was able to pass many quiet evenings in the library teaching himself physics, mechanics and astronomy, and began to produce a string of papers on the motions of the Earth and their effect on climate.

Croll was the first to suggest that cyclical changes in the shape of the Earth's orbit, from elliptical (which is to say, slightly oval) to nearly circular, then back to elliptical again, might explain the advancing and retreating of ice ages.

Ice and wobble

A Serbian mechanical engineer named Milutin Milankovitch took things further. He wondered if there might be a relationship between these complex cycles and the comings and goings of ice ages. Geologists could show that the ice ages of the past had lasted widely different lengths of time – approximately 20,000, 40,000 and 100,000 years respectively. Working out how they came and went and over what periods was going to involve an awful lots of maths.

This was precisely the sort of repetitive work Milankovitch loved. For the next 20 years he worked ceaselessly with pencil and slide rule, computing the tables of his cycles – work that could now be completed in a day or two with a computer. His book, published in 1930, showed there was definitely a relationship between ice ages and planetary wobble.

Summer ice

The Russian–German meteorologist Wladimir Köppen saw that ice ages were caused by cool summers, not brutal winters. If summers are too cool to melt all the snow, more incoming sunlight is bounced back by the reflective white surface, making Earth cooler and encouraging yet more snow to fall. As snow accumulates into an ice sheet, the region grows cooler, leading to more ice.

Mountains of moving ice

Recent ice ages seem pretty small-scale, but of course they were immensely grand by today's standards. At their leading edge, the ice sheets could be nearly 800 metres thick. Imagine standing at the base of a wall of ice that high. Behind this edge, over an area millions of square kilometres large, would be nothing but ice and more ice, with only a few of the tallest mountain summits poking through here and there. Whole continents sagged under the weight of so much ice and even now, 12,000 years after the glaciers' withdrawal, are still rising back into place.

Chilly times

For most of its history until fairly recent times the general pattern for the Earth was to be hot, with no permanent ice anywhere. But now we are living in an ice age which started about 40 million years ago, and has ranged from murderously bad to not bad at all. We live in one of the few spells of the latter.

Our ice age

At the height of the last period of glaciation, around 20,000 years ago, about 30 per cent of the Earth's land surface was under ice; 10 per cent still is. Three-quarters of all the fresh water on Earth is ice even now, and we have ice caps at both Poles – a situation that may be unique in the Earth's history. That there are snowy winters in much of the world, and permanent glaciers even in mild places such as New Zealand, may seem normal, but it's actually most unusual for our planet.

Icy ups and downs

A big freeze occurred about 2.2 billion years ago.

This was followed by a billion years or so of warmth.

Then there was another ice age, even larger than the first, which caused the period known as Snowball Earth. It appears that we've had at least 17 severe glacial episodes in the last 2.5 million years or so.

Some 12,000 years back, Earth began to warm – quite rapidly.

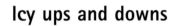

Forecast – more cold on the way

We are now in one of those cycles of comparatively mild weather within ice ages, known as interglacials. In fact, it is only because of this patch of fair weather that humans have been able to develop. But there's no reason to suppose that this warmish climate should last much longer. Some scientists believe we're in for a great deal of cold to come.

It's natural to suppose that global warming might act as a useful balance to the Earth's tendency to plunge back into ice-age conditions. However, global warming could see us melting a lot of ice rather than making it. If all the ice sheets melted, sea levels would rise by 60 metres – the height of a 20-storey building – and every coastal city in the world would be drowned. But the picture is confused: while according to some data, Earth's rise in temperature is starting to cause the meltdown of the West Antarctic ice sheet – in the past 50 years, the waters around it have warmed by 2.5 degrees Celsius – other research suggests a recent *increase* in ice in the Antarctic.

We don't know which is more likely: a future of perishing frigidity or steamy heat. Only one thing is certain: we live on a knife edge.

Ice ages are by no means altogether bad news for the planet. They act as a spur to migration and change. With that in mind, it's time to look at a species of ape that took advantage of this.

Then it abruptly plunged back into bitter cold for a thousand years or so.

After this, Earth warmed up again and we are living in one of its few warmer spells.

However, about 50 more glacial ages can be expected, each lasting around 100,000 years, before we can hope for a really long thaw.

Skull and bones

A model of Java Man, based on fragments of the skull found by Dubois.

Just before Christmas 1887, a young Dutchman, Dr Eugène Dubois, arrived in Sumatra, in the Dutch East Indies. His intention was to find the earliest human remains on Earth. Dubois was simply following a hunch. And what is extraordinary, if not miraculous, is that he found what he was looking for.

A brainy conclusion

Dubois began his search using a team of 50 local convicts. For a year they dug on Sumatra, then moved to the island of Java. And there Dubois – or rather his team, for Dubois himself seldom visited the sites – found a section of ancient human skull. Though only a small part of a skull, it showed that the owner had had distinctly non-human features but also a much larger brain than any ape. Dubois called it *Anthropithecus erectus* and declared it the missing link between apes and humans. It quickly became popularly known as 'Java Man'. Today we know it as *Homo erectus*.

The next year, Dubois' workers found a virtually complete thighbone that looked surprisingly modern. In fact, it probably was but Dubois used the thighbone to suggest – correctly, as it turned out – that *Anthropithecus* walked upright. He also produced, with nothing but a scrap of cranium and one tooth, a model of the complete skull, which also proved uncannily accurate.

Digging around . . .

Half a world away, in late 1924, the small but remarkably complete skull of a child, with an intact face, a lower jaw and a natural cast of the brain, was found on the edge of the Kalahari Desert in Africa. Archaeologists could see at once that this skull was from an earlier, more apelike creature than Java Man. They placed its age at two million years and dubbed it *Australopithecus africanus*, or 'Southern Ape Man of Africa'.

Then, in China, a gifted Canadian amateur named Davidson Black began to poke around at a place called Dragon Bone Hill, which was locally famous as a hunting ground for old bones. He found a single fossilized molar and on the basis of that alone, quite brilliantly, announced the discovery of *Sinanthropus pekinensis*, which quickly became known as 'Peking Man'.

. . . and around

In the following years, as more bones were found, there came a flood of new names – *Homo aurignacensis*, *Australopithecus transvaalensis*, *Paranthropus crassidens*, *Zinjanthropus boisei* and scores of others, nearly all involving a new genus type as well as a new species. By the 1950s, the number of named hominid types had risen to over a hundred.

Where we come from

For the first 99.87 per cent of our history as organisms, we were in the same ancestral line as chimpanzees. Virtually nothing is known about prehistoric chimpanzees, but whatever they were, we were. Then, about seven million years ago, something major happened. A group of new beings emerged from the tropical forests of Africa and began to move about on the open plains. These were the australopithecines.

For the next five million years, the australopithecines would be the world's main hominid species.

Lucy

The most famous australopithecine remains in the world are those of a skeleton dated at 3.18 million years old. It was found in 1974 in Ethiopia and became known as Lucy. Lucy is said by some to be our earliest ancestor, the missing link between apes and humans.

Tiny remains

Lucy was small – just over a metre tall. She could walk, although how well is a matter of argument. She was evidently a good climber too. Much else is unknown. Her skull was almost entirely missing, so little can be said with confidence about her brain size, though skull fragments suggested it was small.

A human body has 206 bones, but many of these are repeated. If you have the left femur from a specimen, you don't need the matching right one too. Lucy has only about 20 per cent of a full skeleton. It isn't even actually known that she was a female, just that she or he was small.

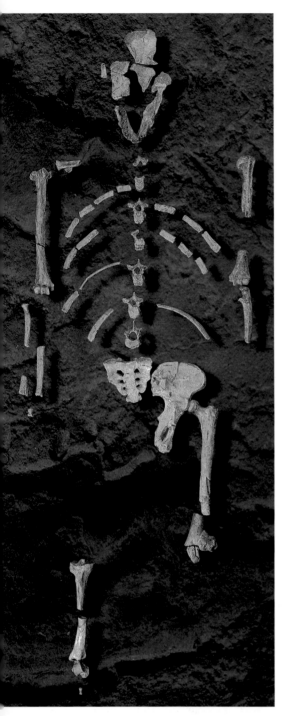

Lucy's skeleton.

There are many who argue about Lucy's real connection to us. More recent finds raise the possibility that creatures like Lucy died out and that another strain proved to be our real ancestors. In 2002, an *Australopithecus* skeleton was dated at almost seven million years old, making it the oldest hominid yet found. It was an early creature and quite primitive, but it walked upright – proof that hominids were doing so far earlier than previously thought.

148

Walking on two legs

Moving from four legs to two legs is demanding and risky. It means you need to refashion the pelvis so it can take the full load of the body. To do this, the birth canal in the female must be comparatively narrow. This has several consequences. First, it means a lot of pain for any mother when giving birth and a greatly increased danger of fatality to both mother and baby. Moreover, to get the baby's head through such a tight space, it must be born while its brain is still small – and while the baby, therefore, is still helpless. This means the infant will need long-term care, which in turn means both male and female must stay together for longer to rear the child.

Facing the dangers

So why did Lucy and her kind come down from the trees and out of the forests? Probably they had no choice. The world was going through a sharp ice age which even affected East Africa, and the thick protection of the jungle was being lost as the region turned into a grassy plain. This left the early hominids far more exposed. Upright hominids could see better, but they were easy prey for any large animal that was stronger, faster and toothier. Under attack, modern humans have only two advantages. We have a good brain and hands with which to fling hurtful objects.

Faced with the need to survive, Lucy and her fellow australopithecines should have developed their intelligence quickly. Yet for over three million years their brain didn't grow and there's no sign that they used even the simplest tools. What is strange is that for about a million years, australopithecines lived alongside other early hominids who *did* use tools.

Big brains

For a long time it was assumed that big brains and upright walking were directly related, but fossil evidence of australopithecines showed there was no connection at all. Indeed, the rise of a big brain may simply have been an evolutionary accident.

Skull of *Homo sapiens neanderthalensis*

Skull of *Homo erectus*

Skull of *Homo habilis*

Skull of *Homo australopithecus*

Huge brains are demanding organs: they make up only 2% of the body's mass, but use up 20% of its energy. Brains are also comparatively picky in what they use as fuel. They need glucose, and lots of it, and if the brain goes hungry, it rapidly leads to death.

Absolute brain size doesn't tell you everything. Elephants and whales both have brains larger than ours. It's brain size relative to body size that matters.

From there to here

At one point between three million and two million years ago, it appears there may have been as many as six types of *Australopithecus* very like Lucy co-existing in Africa. Only one was fated to last, *Homo*, which emerged about two million years ago. All australopithecines vanished mysteriously over a million years ago.

Homo habilis

The *Homo* line begins with *Homo habilis*, a creature about whom we know almost nothing. *Homo habilis* ('handy man') was so called because it was the first hominid to use tools, albeit very simple ones. It was a fairly primitive creature, much more chimpanzee than human, but its brain was about 50 per cent larger than that of Lucy.

Homo erectus

Homo erectus is the dividing line: everything that came before him was apelike in character; everything that came after him was humanlike. *Homo erectus* existed from about 1.8 million years ago to possibly as recently as 20,000 or so years ago. *Homo erectus* was the first to hunt, the first to use fire, the first to fashion complex tools, the first to leave evidence of campsites, the first to look after the weak and frail.

Homo erectus

Homo habilis

Australopithecus afarensis

Compared with all that had gone before, *Homo erectus* was extremely human in form as well as behaviour: its limbs were long and lean, it was very strong (much stronger than modern humans), and had the drive and intelligence to spread successfully over huge areas.

Homo sapiens neanderthalensis

Neanderthals were nothing if not tough. For tens of thousands of years, they lived through the worst of the ice ages when blizzards with hurricane-force winds were common. Temperatures routinely fell to minus 45 degrees Celsius, and polar bears padded across the snowy vales of southern England. A Neanderthal who lived much past 30 was lucky indeed – but as a species they were magnificently resilient and practically indestructible. They survived across an area stretching from Gibraltar to Uzbekistan, which is a pretty successful run for any species.

Homo sapiens

These early modern humans are surprisingly shadowy. Their first undisputed appearance is in the eastern Mediterranean about 100,000 years ago.

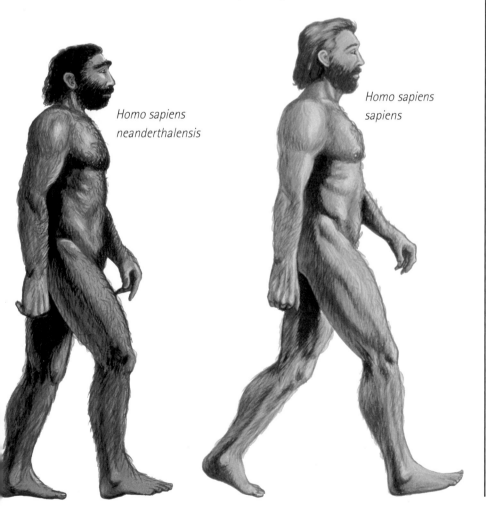

Homo sapiens neanderthalensis

Homo sapiens sapiens

It is worth remembering that all of these evolutionary jostlings, from distant *Australopithecus* to fully modern human, produced a creature that is genetically 98.4% the same as the modern chimpanzee.

Tool-makers

Some time about a million and a half years ago, a forgotten genius of the hominid world did an unexpected thing. He (or very possibly she) took one stone and carefully used it to shape another. The result was a simple teardrop-shaped hand-axe, but it was the world's first piece of advanced technology.

Acheulean tools

It was so superior to existing tools that, soon, others were following the inventor's lead and making hand-axes of their own. Eventually, whole societies existed that seemed to do little else. The axes became known as Acheulean tools, after a place in northern France where the first examples were found. They contrast with the older, simpler tools known as Oldowan, originally found at Olduvai Gorge in Tanzania, East Africa.

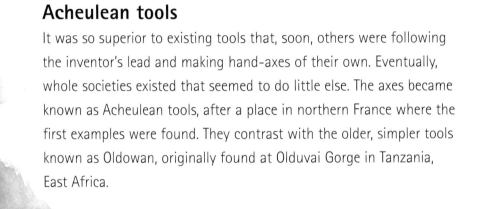

A tool factory

In the Great Rift Valley, which arcs across nearly 5,000 kilometres of East Africa, is an ancient site called Olorgesailie. Here, where there was once a large lake, tools were made in incalculable numbers. The quartz and obsidian rocks from which the axes were made were carried from mountains about 10 kilometres away – a long way to carry an armload of stone.

Sharp practice

The tool-makers then organized the site so there were areas where axes were fashioned and others where blunt axes were brought to be resharpened. The axes were tricky and labour-intensive objects to make. Even with practice, each one would take hours to fashion – and yet, curiously, they were not particularly good for cutting or chopping or scraping or any other tasks. Oddly, these early people appeared to gather in large numbers at this particular site to make tools that were rather bad at the job.

Humans on the move

The traditional theory to explain how we all relate to these early humans – and the one still accepted by the majority of people in the field – is that they spread from Africa in two waves.

The first wave consisted of *Homo erectus,* who left Africa remarkably quickly – almost as soon as they emerged as a species – beginning nearly two million years ago. Over time, as they settled in different regions, these early erect people evolved further into *Anthropithecus erectus* and *Sinanthropus pekinensis* in Asia, and finally the Neanderthals in Europe.

Then, over 100,000 years ago, a smarter species of creature arose on the African plains and began radiating outwards in a second wave. Wherever they went, these new *Homo sapiens* displaced their less clever predecessors. These were the ancestors of every one of us today.

So, we got here!

We started off by not knowing much about salty oceans, and now we know an awful lot more about this and a great many other topics too. Congratulations for staying with it and I hope you are enjoying your new knowledge. Given that we started 3.8 billion years ago, we have indeed come a long way.

What we know so far:

- Life on this planet has been constantly changing for billions of years.
- Our ancestors had the power (and luck) to survive, which is why we are here.
- We started as single-cell organisms.
- We needed the qualities of our unique planet, with its mix of gases, moisture and warmth, to accomplish even that.
- We changed over and over again to get to our present dominant hominid state.

Where did we come from?

For 3.8 billion years
some kind of life has been around on our planet.

640 million years ago
The earliest known creatures appear.

540 million years ago
Trilobites first appear.

400 million years ago
The first land creatures arrive from the sea.

At least 7 million years ago
The first hominids appear.

What are we made of?
1730s Carolus Linnaeus sets about classifying all the living things found on the planet.

1858 Charles Darwin publishes *On the Origin of Species*, which suggests that species that survive are those best equipped to cope with changing environments.

1865 Gregor Mendel presents his discoveries, which reveal the secret of hereditary traits.

1908 Thomas Hunt Morgan is able to confirm that chromosomes are at the heart of our genetic make-up.

1953 Watson and Crick unravel the shape of a DNA molecule: the famous double helix.

Earth's ice ages

1860 James Croll suggests that changes in the shape of the Earth's orbit might explain the advancing and retreating of ice ages.

1930 Milutin Milankovitch carries out copious mathematical equations and is able to confirm Croll's theory.

Our hominid ancestors

1891 Marie Eugène François Thomas Dubois finds a section of ancient human skull, which he calls *Anthropithecus erectus*.

1974 The most famous australopithecine remains are found in Ethiopia and become known as Lucy.

Australopithecus

lived between three million and two million years ago.

Homo habilis was a fairly primitive creature, much more chimpanzee than human, and lived from about two million years ago.

Homo erectus

appeared about 1.8 million years ago. *Homo erectus* was the first to hunt, the first to use fire, the first to fashion complex tools and make campsites.

Homo sapiens neanderthalensis

appeared over 100,000 years ago. They were tough and survived thousands of years of the worst of the ice ages.

Given how difficult it was to get here, you might think we would want to protect the planet that made us . . . but we're not doing a great job.

Humans take over

The famously flightless dodo.

We don't know the date or precise circumstances which led to the last moments of the very last dodo, but we do know it's difficult to excuse the pounding into extinction of a creature that never did us any harm.

A lost record

What is known of the dodo is this: it lived on Mauritius, was plump but not tasty, and was the biggest-ever member of the pigeon family. Being flightless, it nested on the ground, leaving its eggs and chicks as tragically easy prey for pigs, dogs and monkeys brought to the island by outsiders. Indeed, dodos were so short on insight, it's reported that if you wished to find all the dodos in a neighbourhood, you had only to catch one and set it squawking and all the others would waddle along to see what was up.

It was certainly extinct by 1693. But the indignities heaped on the poor dodo didn't end there. In 1755, some 70 years after the last dodo's death, the director of the Ashmolean Museum in Oxford, UK, decided that their stuffed dodo was starting to smell musty and tossed it on a bonfire. This was the only dodo in existence, stuffed or otherwise, so today we're not even completely sure what a dodo looked like.

Going, going, gone

Altogether, North and South America between them lost about three-quarters of their big animals once hunting peoples arrived with their flint-headed spears. Europe and Asia, where the animals had had longer to become wary of humans, lost between a third and a half of their big creatures. Australia lost no less than 95 per cent

Hunters have shot hundreds of thousands of animals in the quest for trophy horns and tusks.

Strange beasts

Some of the creatures that were lost were spectacular and would take a little managing if they were still around. Imagine ground sloths that could look into an upstairs window, tortoises nearly the size of a small car, monitor lizards six metres long basking beside desert highways in Western Australia. Today, across the whole world, only four types of really hefty land animals survive: elephants, rhinos, hippos and giraffes. Not for tens of millions of years has life on Earth been so small and tame.

The impulse to exterminate continued into recent times. In Australia, bounties were paid on the Tasmanian tiger, or thylacine – a doglike creature with distinctive 'tiger' stripes across its back – until shortly before the last one died, forlorn and nameless, in a private Hobart zoo in 1936. Go to the Tasmanian Museum and Art Gallery today and ask to see the last of this species – the only large carnivorous marsupial to live into modern times – and all they can show you are photographs and 61 seconds of old film footage. Upon its death, the last thylacine was thrown out with the weekly trash.

Killer species?

So, are humans bad news for other living things? The sad likelihood is that we may well be. The natural rate of extinction on Earth throughout biological history has been one species lost every four years on average. According to some, human-caused extinction may now be running at as much as 120,000 times that level.

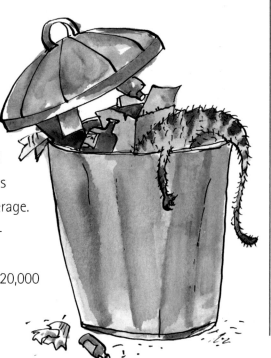

The Chatham Islands swan simply disappeared, leaving almost no trace.

The Chatham Islands swan

Steller's sea cow, a walrus-like creature, became extinct in the mid-1700s.

Steller's sea cow

The Carolina parakeet was hunted to extinction by American farmers who thought it a pest.

The Carolina parakeet

Nobody knows quite how destructive human beings are. But it's a fact that over the last 50,000 years or so, wherever we have gone, animals have tended to vanish in astonishingly large numbers.

What now?

We have traced the progress of our planet from its creation at the nano-second of the Big Bang to the moment where our ancestors began to dominate its surface. At this point, its history, as far as humans were concerned, was all to come. But after several million years of human occupation, just what have we got now?

Overrun

Unfortunately, human beings like Thomas Midgley seem to take a careless pleasure in disrupting their planet. With each passing decade, there are, of course, many more millions of us struggling to find a patch on it, while for some the struggle is one of day-to-day survival rather than adding to one's pool of comforts.

Dangerous demands

The end result of our demand for more and better, more and faster, is that we are putting lots of extra carbon dioxide into the atmosphere. Since 1850, it's been estimated we have lofted about 100 billion tonnes of extra carbon dioxide into the air, a total that increases by about seven billion tonnes each year. Overall, that's not actually all that much. Nature – mostly through the belchings of volcanoes and the decay of plants – sends about 200 billion tonnes of carbon dioxide into the atmosphere each year – nearly 30 times as much as we do with our cars and factories. But you have only to look at the haze of pollution that hangs over our cities to see that our contribution adds to things.

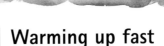

Warming up fast

So far, the Earth's oceans and forests (which also pack away a lot of carbon) have managed to save us from ourselves. But there's a critical point at which Nature will stop buffering us from the effects of our emissions and actually start to make things worse. The fear is that there will be a very rapid increase in the Earth's warming. Unable to adapt, many trees and other plants will die, releasing their stores of carbon and adding to the problem.

The good news is that the last time life was virtually annihilated on our planet, it got back on its feet again.

The bad news is that it took 60,000 years to do so, which means not one of us would be around to enjoy it.

Goodbye

I mention all this to make the point that if you were designing an organism to look after life in our lonely cosmos, to monitor where it is going and keep a record of where it has been, you wouldn't choose human beings for the job.

The best there is

However, we have been chosen – by fate or providence, or whatever you wish to call it. As far as we can tell, we are the best there is. We may be *all* there is. It's an unnerving thought that we may be the living universe's supreme achievement and its worst nightmare at one and the same time.

Because we're so remarkably careless about looking after things, both when they're alive and when they're not, we have no idea – really none at all – about how many things have died off permanently, or may do so soon, or may never, and what role we have played in any part of the process.

The fact is, we don't have any real idea how our present actions will affect the future. What we do know is that we have just one planet to inhabit, and we are the only species on it capable of deciding its future.

The luck of the draw

To attain any kind of life at all in this universe of ours appears to be quite an achievement. As humans we are doubly lucky, of course. We enjoy not only the privilege of existence, but also the singular ability to appreciate it and even, in a multitude of ways, to make it better. It's a trick we have only just begun to grasp.

We have arrived at this position of eminence in a stunningly short time. Behaviourally modern humans have been around for less than 0.01 per cent of Earth's history – almost nothing really – but even existing for that short while has required a nearly endless string of good fortune.

We really are at the beginning of it all. The trick, of course, is to make sure we never find the end. And that will require a lot more than a series of lucky breaks.

Index

A

Acheulean tools 152

acids 106, 108, 123

adenosine triphosphate 117

AIDS (acquired immune deficiency syndrome) 113

air pressure 98–9

alchemy 58

algae 101, 108–9, 119, 123

aliens 20–22

Alpha Centauri 23

aluminium 59

Alvarez, Luis and Walter 90–91, 114

amber 21

amino acids 106–7, 111

ammonia 106

ammonites 47

amoebas 109

anaesthetic 58

ancestors, ancestry 119, 126, 137–8, 148, 153

anchisaurus 51

Andromeda constellation 68

Anning, Mary 47, 74

Antarctic(a) 29, 71, 100, 103, 123

antennas 10–11, 120

Anthropithecus 146, 153, 155

antibiotics 111

archaea 109

Arctic 100

arsenic 61

arthropods 121

asteroid belt 15

asteroids 14, 90, 92–3, 114–15

Astronomer Royal 34–5

astronomers 10, 16–17, 26, 33–4, 64, 67–9

astronomy 32–3, 69, 142

Atlantic Ocean 80–81, 100, 103

atmosphere 7, 17, 63, 70–71, 73–4, 91–2, 95–101, 108–9, 114, 159

atomic bomb 85

atomic weight 57

atoms 4, 8–9, 40, 56–8, 60, 71–2, 74, 102, 107, 117

ATP (adenosine triphosphate) 117

australopithecines, *Australopithecus* 147–51, 155

avalanches 85

B

bacteria 37, 108–15

bdelloid rotifers 133

Beagle, HMS 134

Becher, Johann 58

Becquerel, Henri 62

Bell Laboratories 10

bends (the) 105

Big Bang 5–7, 10–11, 38

Big Bone Lick 51

Black, Davidson 147

black holes 16, 36

Bone Cabin Quarry 55

bones 47, 50–51, 74, 121, 124, 135, 141, 147–8

botanists 130–31, 137

Bouguer, Pierre 30–31, 38

brain size 149

Brand, Hennig 58

brontosaurus 53

Buckland, William 42–3, 54

Buffon, Comte de 50

Burgess Shale 120, 122

C

calcium 9, 59, 80

calderas 86–7

calories 94

Cambrian period 48–9, 54, 120

carbon 9, 72, 106, 159

carbon-14 72

carbon dating 72

carbon dioxide 7, 71, 159

Carboniferous period 48

Carolina parakeet 157

catastrophism 44

Cavendish, Henry 36–7, 39

cells 105, 107–10, 113, 116–17, 139–41

Cenozoic era 48–9

centipedes 133

centrifugal force 28

CFCs (chlorofluorocarbons) 71, 75

chalk 101

Chappe, Jean 32

Chatham Islands swan 157

chemicals 7, 62, 102, 106, 140

chemistry 9, 55–61, 70, 102

chemists 58, 60, 62, 74

chimpanzees 147, 150–51

chlorine 58

chordata 131

Christiansen, Bob 86–7

Christy, James 16

chromosomes 137, 139

circumference (of Earth) 27, 30, 38

cirrus 99

clams 40–41

Clark, William 51

classification 130

climate 100, 142

clouds 99

coal 46, 122, 125

coccoliths 101

comets 7, 14–15, 24–5, 91, 128

continental plates 45, 78–9, 115

continents 41, 76–9, 114

contour lines 35

convection 82, 98

Cook, James 33

Cope, Edward 53

coprolites 43

coral reefs 134

core (Earth's) 3, 7, 82–3

cosmic radiation 11, 38, 95

cosmic rays 96–7

cosmologists 5

craters 87, 90–91

Cretaceous period 48–9, 52, 128

Crick, Francis 140, 155

Croll, James 142, 155

crust (Earth's) 45, 72, 78–9, 81–2, 114

crustaceans 105, 121, 124

cryptozoa 132

Crystal Palace Park 52–3

crystals 72–3

cumulus 99

Curie, Marie and Pierre 62–3, 75

Cuvier, Georges 51, 74

cyanobacteria 108–9

cytoplasm 117

cytoskeleton 117

D

Dalton, John 57, 74

Darwin, Charles 54, 134–8, 154

Davy, Humphry 59

deoxyribonucleic acid (DNA) 107, 139–41, 155

Devonian period 48, 128

dinosaurs 47, 50–55, 90–91, 95, 114, 122, 126–7

diplodocus 53

diseases 112–13

diving 104–5

diving bell 24

Dixon, Jeremiah 34

DNA (deoxyribonucleic acid) 107, 139–41, 155

dodo 156

Doppler, Johann Christian 67

Doppler shift 67

Dover, White Cliffs of 101

Dragon Bone Hill 147

dragonflies 125

Drake, Frank 21

Dubois, Eugène 146, 155

E

Earth 6–7, 15, 25–9, 31–41, 44–5, 54–5, 63, 72–84, 88, 91–7, 99, 101, 103, 106–9, 114, 118–19, 121–3, 128–9, 142–5, 155, 159, 161

earthquakes 3, 36, 41, 79, 82, 84–5, 87–9, 114–15

Einstein, Albert 56, 64–6, 68, 75

electricity 56, 59, 63

electrolysis 59

electromagnetism 6

electrons 6, 23, 56

elements 5, 9, 57–61, 74–5, 103, 106

ellipses 24

energy 16, 23, 62–4, 75

Eocene period 49

Equator 28–9, 31, 98

erosion 40, 80

eukaryota 131

European Space Agency 29

Evans, Reverend Robert 22–3

evolution 119, 151

exosphere 96–7

extinctions 44, 90, 120, 127–9, 156–7

F

ferns 121, 125

fish 45, 124, 126, 131

floods 40–41

foraminiferans 101

fossils 40, 43, 45–7, 50–55, 63, 74, 76, 91, 109, 120–21, 123, 126–7, 134, 147

fruit flies 139

fungi 109, 123, 131

G

galaxies 7, 11, 16, 20, 22, 67–9, 74–5

Gamow, George 11

gases 7, 60–61, 63, 68, 71, 95, 97, 106, 108, 114, 128, 154

genes 137–9, 154

Geological Society 42–3, 74

geologists 35, 41–2, 45, 49, 54–5, 64, 74, 76, 78, 88, 90, 107, 142

geology 41–9, 54, 74, 84

geophysicists 81

geysers 86–7

giant ground sloths 51, 134

glaciers 45, 144

Global Positioning Systems 79

global warming 128, 145, 159

granite 121

gravity 5–6, 25, 29, 34, 36–9, 65–6, 93

Great Kanto earthquake 89

Great Rift Valley 153

greenhouse gases 7, 101

Gulf Stream 100

Gutenberg, Beno 88, 114

H

hadrocodium 126

hadrosaur 50

Halley, Edmond 24, 32, 38–9

Halley's comet 17, 24

hand-axes 152–3

helium 5, 61

high-pressure systems 99

Hipparchus 26

hipparion 77

HIV 113

HMS *Beagle* 134

hominids 131, 147–9, 152, 154–5

Homo erectus 146, 149–51, 153, 155

Homo habilis 149–50, 155

Homo sapiens 131, 149, 151, 153, 155

horses 77, 129

hot springs 86–7

Howard, Luke 99

Hubble, Edwin 68–9, 75

Hubble Space Telescope 18, 69, 91

hurricanes 98, 128, 151

Hutton, Charles 35, 39

Hutton, James 40–41, 44–5, 74

hydrogen 5, 9, 57, 59, 61, 102, 106, 108

hydrogen bomb 64

hydrogen peroxide 60

hylaeosaurus 52

I

ice 99, 102, 143–4

ice ages 45, 95, 142–5, 149, 151, 155

ice sheets 72, 91, 143, 145

ichthyosaur 47

iguanodon 52

illness 112–13

Indian Ocean 29, 79, 103

infection 112–13

inflation theory 7

inheritance 137, 139

insects 121–2, 128, 131

iron 2, 7, 57, 106

J

Java Man 146–7

Jupiter 15, 19, 91

Jurassic period 48–9, 127

K

Kelvin, William Thomson, Lord 54

Köppen, Wladimir 143

KT boundary 91

KT extinction 129

Kuiper belt 17

L

La Condamine, Charles Marie de 30, 38

Lalande, Joseph 33

land bridges 77

landslides 85

Lascaux caves 72

Lavoisier, Antoine-Laurent 59

Le Gentil, Guillaume 33

lead 70, 72–3, 75

lead poisoning 70

Leavitt, Henrietta Swan 68

Lewis, Meriwether 51

Libby, Willard 72

lichens 123

light 13, 23, 64–5, 67

light years 13, 21, 68

lightning 98–9, 106, 108

limestone 90, 101

Linnaeus, Carolus 130–31, 154

Lisbon earthquake 89, 115

lizards 52

longitude 27

low-pressure systems 98–9

Lowell Observatory 16

Lucy 148–50, 155

Lyell, Charles 42–5, 48, 75

lystrosaurus 77

M

magma 45, 83, 87, 95

magnesium 59

magnetic fields 83, 95

magnetism 24, 63, 83

mammals 45, 94, 122–3, 126–7, 129, 131

mammoths 51

manganese 58

Manson crater 90–91, 115

Mantell, Gideon Algernon 52

mantle (Earth's) 7, 82–3

maps 46, 48

Marat, Jean-Paul 59

Mariana Trench 105, 115

Mars 18, 92, 94

Marsh, Othniel Charles 53

marsupials 76, 157

Maskelyne, Nevil 34–5, 39

Mason, Charles 34–5

mastodon 51, 74

mathematics 24, 65, 136, 142, 155

Matthews, Drummond 81, 114

megalonyx 51

megalosaurus 53

megatherium 134

Mendel, Gregor 136–7, 154

Mendeleyev, Dmitri Ivanovich 60–61, 75

Mercury 16

meridian 27, 38

mesosphere 97

Mesozoic era 48–9

metals 58, 60–61

meteorites 73

meteoroids 14

meteorologists 100, 143

meteorology 99

meteors 7, 73, 92, 128

methane 7, 106, 128

Michell, John 36–7, 39

microbes 109–12, 114, 122, 133

microns 57

microwaves 11

Midgley, Thomas Junior 70–71, 75, 158

Milankovitch, Milutin 142, 155

Milky Way 20–21, 69

millipedes 125

minerals 42, 46, 90, 110, 121, 123, 131

mines 82

Miocene period 48–9

mites 124, 132

mitochondria 109

molecules 56, 71, 102–3, 107–8, 116, 121

monera 131

Moody, Plinus 51

Moon 7, 16–18, 20, 22, 26, 35, 93, 95, 111

moons 14–16, 18, 35

Morgan, Thomas Hunt 139, 154

mosquitoes 112

Mount St Helens 84–5, 115

Murchison, Roderick 43, 49

N

NASA (National Aeronautics and Space Agency) 17, 71, 87

naturalists 51, 135

Neanderthals 135, 149, 151, 153, 155

nebulae 9

Neptune 18

Neptunists 41, 44

neutron stars 23

neutrons 6, 23, 56, 60

Newton, Sir Isaac 24-5, 28-9, 31, 34, 36-8, 57

nickel 2

nimbus 99

nitrogen 7, 9, 58, 104-6, 111

nitrous oxide 58

Norwood, Richard 27, 38

nucleotides 111

nucleus 23, 56, 60, 139

Nucleus G 91

O

obsidian 153

ocean tides 25

oceanographers 81

oceans 7, 76-7, 79-82, 99-106, 114-15

okapis 133

Oldowan tools 152

Olduvai Gorge 152

Oligocene period 49

Olorgesailie 153

Oort cloud 15, 18

orbits 6-7, 17, 24-5, 37, 90, 92-3, 142, 155

Ordovician period 48, 128

ores 63

organisms 56, 101, 108-9, 112-13, 123, 127, 133, 160

Origin of Species, On the 135, 154

Owen, Richard 52

oxygen 9, 57-9, 71, 96-7, 106, 108-9, 124

ozone 71

P

Pacific Ocean 3, 29, 79-80, 103, 105

Palaeocene period 49

palaeontology 51, 53, 55

Palaeozoic era 48-9

Pangaea 76, 114, 124

Parkinson, James 43

particles 4, 8, 57, 65, 96-7, 109

Patterson, Clair 72-3, 75

Peking Man 147

Penzias, Arno 10-11

Periodic Table 60-61, 75

Permian period 46, 49, 128

pesticides 70

petrol 70

Philosophiae Naturalis Principia Mathematica 24-5, 38, 57

phosphorus 58, 106

photons 11

physics 5-6, 63, 142

pitchblende 63

planetesimals 6

planets 6, 9, 14-17, 21, 24-5, 32, 35, 38, 40, 63, 91, 94

plate tectonics 41, 45, 78-9, 82, 95, 114

Pleistocene period 48-9

plesiosaurus 47

Plutinos 17

Pluto 14-18, 38

Plutonists 41, 44

plutonium 57

poisons 58, 61, 70, 103, 108

Poles, North and South 27, 31, 103

pollution 159

polonium 62

potassium 59

Precambrian era and period 48-9, 123

predators 124

pressure 96, 105, 115

primates 131

Principles of Geology, The 45

proteins 106-7, 141

protists (see also protozoans) 131

protons 3-4, 6, 56, 60

protoplasm 118

protozoans 109, 131-2

Proxima Centauri 20

pterodactyl 47

Q

quartz 90, 153

quasars 3, 11, 16

R

radiation 11, 63-4, 75, 95, 124

radiation sickness 62

radioactivity 62-3, 72

radium 62-3

radium bromide 63

rainforests 132

red-shift 67, 75

refrigerators 71

Relativity, Special Theory of 64–5, 75
reptiles 45, 52, 126, 129, 131
ribonucleic acid (RNA) 141
ribosomes 141
Richter, Charles 88, 114
Richter scale 88–9, 114
riwoche 133
rock dating 46, 48–50, 74
rock strata 46, 48
Russell, Bertrand 65
Rutherford, Ernest 63

S

salt 3, 100, 103
satellites 29, 71, 93
Saturn 19
Scheele, Karl 58
Schiehallion, mountain 34–6, 39
sea level 41, 56, 128
Sedgwick, Adam 49
sediment 80–81, 121
sedimentary rocks 120
seismic 89
seismologists 84
Shakespeare, William 56, 138
Shoemaker, Eugene 90, 114
singularity 4
Silurian period 48–9
Sinanthropus pekinensis 147, 153
slime moulds 109
Slipher, Vesto 67–8, 75
smallpox 113
Smith, William 46, 74

Snowball Earth 144
sodium 59
soil 40, 99
solar flares 128
solar winds 97
solar system 6, 14–20, 32, 35, 38, 73–4, 101
space 11–16, 20–21, 66–7, 90
space probe 19
space travel 18
spacetime 66
species 127–8, 130–32, 134–6, 138, 147, 151, 153–4
spectographs 67
spectrums 67, 69, 75
speed of light 13, 64
speed of sound 91
sponges 117
stars 7, 9, 15–16, 18, 20–23, 56, 64, 67–8, 75
stegosaurus 53
Steller's sea cow 157
stratosphere 71, 96
stratus 99
streptococcus 111
stromatolites 109
strontium 59
sulphur 7, 9
Sun 2, 6–7, 14–15, 17–18, 23–4, 32–3, 35, 39–40, 63, 66, 71, 82–3, 95, 97, 99, 101, 142
supernovae 22–3, 38
surface tension 103
swamps 125

T

takahe 133
tapirs 77
Tasmanian tiger 157
taxonomy 130
Taylor, Frank Bursley 78, 114
tectonic plates 41, 45, 78–9, 89, 114
telescopes 18, 22, 36–7, 69, 91
temperature 96–7, 114, 145, 151
tetrapods 126
thermosphere 96–7
thunderstorms 99
thylacine 157
titanis 129
Tokyo earthquake 89, 115
Tombaugh, Clyde 17
tools 149–50, 152–3, 155
triangulation 26–7, 32, 38–9
Triassic period 48–9, 77, 128
triceratops 53
trigonometry 27
trilobites 76, 114, 120–22, 128
troposphere 96–8
tsunamis 89, 92
tusks 51
tyrannosaurus 128

U

ultraviolet radiation 71, 124
universal law of gravitation 25
universe 3–7, 9, 11–13, 16, 21, 25, 38, 56, 61, 64–5, 67–9, 75, 94–5, 111, 161

uranium 62–4, 72–3

urine 58

Ussher, James 54

V

Varuna 17

vents 87

Venus 32–4, 39, 94

Vine, Fred 81, 114

viruses 109, 113

volcanoes 81–2, 84–7, 92, 115

Voyager 14–15, 18–19

W

Walcott, Charles Doolittle
120–21

Wallace, Alfred Russel 135

water 99, 102–4

water cycle 102

water pressure 104–5

water vapour 103

Watson, James 140, 155

weather 3, 24, 96, 98–100,

Wegener, Alfred 76, 114

white blood cells 108, 113

Wilson, Robert 10–11

Wistar, Caspar 50

Wolbachia 112

woodlice 124

worms 131

Wren, Sir Christopher 24

X

X-rays 2, 139

Y

yeasts 116

Yellowstone National Park 86–7,
115

Z

Zwicky, Fritz 23

Picture Credits

Stuart Abraham/Alamy: 158bl.

Alinari/Topfoto: 72tl.

Douglas Allen/istockphoto: 112bl.

American Museum of Natural History: 55tr.

Galyna Andrushko/istockphoto: 30–31b.

Chuck Babbit/istockphoto: 100bl.

Tom Bean/Getty Images: 127

Blackbeck/istockphoto: 103br.

Gary Braasch/Corbis: 87tr.

British Geological Survey: 46t.

Bill Bryson: 2t

Adrian Chinery/Alamy: 53b.

Clark et al/McDonald Observatory/SPL: 91cr.

CNRI/SPL: 111tr.

Stephen Coburn/Shutterstock: 47c.

Phil Degginger/Carnegie Museum/Alamy: 46b, 74bl.

DK Images: 79cr, 139b.

ESA: 28–9c,

ESA and G. Bacon (STScI)/NASA: 16bl.

ESA/JHU/APL/HST/NASA: 16–17c, 38bl.

Mary Evans PL: 136tl.

Jeff Foot/Getty Images: 121bl

John Foster/SPL: 73b.

Fox Photos/Hulton Archive/Getty: 52tl.

Getty Images: 64tl

David Gifford/SPL: 150–51b.

Yves Grau/istockphoto: 47tr.

Julien Grondin/istockphoto: 83r, 115tr.

Jaap Hart/istockphoto: 159–8.

Doug Houghton/Topfoto: 34–5.

G. Huedepohl: 143.

istockphotos: 64cl, 120tl.

JPL/NASA: 15tr, 18–19.

JSC/NASA: 68–9.

Nancy Kedersha/Getty Images: 117b

Masanori Kobayashi/Alamy: 85b.

O. Krause/Steward Observatory/JPL-Caltech/NASA: 22–3c, 39tr.

David Muench/Corbis: 40tl, 84tl.

NASA: 6–7, 10b, 14t, 17br, 29cr, 66–7, 75tr, 92–3, 94bl, 95tr, 96–7b, 102tl.

NOAA: 98bl.

Shigemi Numazawa/Japan Planetarium Lab: 32tl.

James Osmond/Alamy: 44–5t.

Dr David M. Phillips/Getty Images: 116tl

Valeriy Poltorak/Shutterstock: 84–5.

Radiation Protection Division/Health Protection Agency/SPL: 63tr.

J. C. Revy/SPL: 72bl.

Science & Society PL: 140bl.

Sciencephotos/Alamy: 67tr.

Franck Seguin/TempSport/Corbis: 104bl.

Shutterstock: 62–3.

Soubrette/istockphoto: 98–9r.

Studio City/Alamy: 86cl.

SVS TOMS/NASA: 71br.

Sheila Terry/SPL: 146tl.

Javier Trueba/MSF/SPL: 148tl.

Valentina Volkov/stockphotos: 136t.

ADULT BOOKS BY BILL BRYSON

Bill Bryson's African Diary
Bill Bryson goes to Kenya at the invitation of CARE International and casts his inimitable eye on a continent new to him.
"Bryson has become an enormously popular travel writer by coming off as the most literate tour guide you've ever had."—*The New York Times*

Bryson's Dictionary for Writers and Editors
An indispensable companion to all those who write, work with the written word, or just enjoy getting things right.
"Bryson's erudition is evident and refreshing . . . a straightforward, concise, utilitarian guide."—*Publishers Weekly*

In a Sunburned Country
Bill Bryson journeys to Australia and promptly falls in love with the country. And who can blame him?
"Vastly entertaining. . . . If there is one book with which to get oriented before departure or en route to Australia, this is it."—*The New York Times*

The Life and Times of the Thunderbolt Kid
Quintessential Bryson—a funny, moving and perceptive journey through his childhood.
"Bill Bryson's laugh-out-loud pilgrimage through his fifties childhood in heartland America is a national treasure. It's full of insights, wit, and wicked adolescent fantasies."—Tom Brokaw

The Lost Continent
A classic of travel literature—hilariously, stomach-achingly funny, yet tinged with heartache—and the book that first staked Bill Bryson's claim as the most beloved writer of his generation.
"Funny, biting, outrageous, and more truthful than we may care to admit."—*Detroit Free Press*

Made in America
Bill Bryson takes a fast, exhilarating ride along the Route 66 of American language and popular culture.
"A treat . . . filled with surprises . . . a literate exploration of why we use—or mangle—our native tongue."—*USA Today*

Neither Here nor There
Bill Bryson brings his unique brand of humor to bear on Europe as he shoulders his backpack.
"This book is fun for travelers or armchair travelers, especially for anyone who journeyed through Europe in the hippie days of the early 1970s."—*School Library Journal*

I'm a Stranger Here Myself
Bryson turns his inimitable wit to that strangest of phenomena: the American way of life.
"Painfully funny and genuinely insightful . . . Bryson has never been wittier or more endearing."—*San Francisco Chronicle*

Notes from a Small Island
A eulogy for Bryson's beloved Britain captures the very essence of the original "green and pleasant land."
"Bryson shares what he loves best about the idiosyncrasies of everyday English life in this immensely entertaining travel memoir."—*Publishers Weekly*

A Short History of Nearly Everything
"Stylish [and] stunningly accurate prose. We learn what the material world is like from the smallest quark to the largest galaxy and at all the levels in between . . . brims with strange and amazing facts . . . destined to become a modern classic of science writing."—*The New York Times*

A Short History of Nearly Everything (Illustrated)

A Walk in the Woods
Bryson's punishing (by his standards) hike along the celebrated Appalachian Trail, the longest continuous footpath in the world.
"Choke-on-your-coffee funny."—*The Washington Post Book World*